Choices

Verné's Vignettes

DeeVerné

authorHOUSE

AuthorHouse™
1663 Liberty Drive
Bloomington, IN 47403
www.authorhouse.com
Phone: 833-262-8899

© 2023 DeeVerné. All rights reserved.

No part of this book may be reproduced, stored in a retrieval system, or transmitted by any means without the written permission of the author.

Published by AuthorHouse 09/07/2023

ISBN: 979-8-8230-1344-4 (sc)
ISBN: 979-8-8230-1342-0 (hc)
ISBN: 979-8-8230-1343-7 (e)

Library of Congress Control Number: 2023915547

Print information available on the last page.

Any people depicted in stock imagery provided by Getty Images are models, and such images are being used for illustrative purposes only.
Certain stock imagery © Getty Images.

This book is printed on acid-free paper.

Because of the dynamic nature of the Internet, any web addresses or links contained in this book may have changed since publication and may no longer be valid. The views expressed in this work are solely those of the author and do not necessarily reflect the views of the publisher, and the publisher hereby disclaims any responsibility for them.

Here are my thoughts, memories, lessons, and actions in no specific order. There will be flashbacks of good times, feelings of sadness and regret, fits of rage, and a love story, all in one. There is a little bit of everyone somewhere in these short stories.

Mommy,

Let me start by saying thank you. Thank you for being the best mother I could ever ask for. It's not easy sharing you with the world; I always want to protect you and keep you safe.

You have supported my ideas and actions; even when you didn't agree, you gave me a hundred percent. Thank you for being a friend and my biggest cheerleader. You are picture-perfect, selfless! I want to let you know that not one day has gone by that I haven't appreciated you and all that you have done for me and with me. Even when your glass is half-full, you find a way to fill mine. How awesome is that! Just know that you are a blessing to me, and I thank God for giving me to you. You are truly my sunshine.

Love,
Verne'

Through My Eyes and Footsteps

"Why? Why can't I go? Can I go off the block and visit family with my brother on my own?"

"For what?" would be my parents' response. "What is the reason you want to go?" "Maybe another day." "Wait until tomorrow." "You're not old enough." Or my all-time favorite: "Because I said so." My silent thoughts were about how I just wanted to find my way and feel like I had some say in what I did day to day.

Things I missed because of the word *no*:

- Trouble in the streets
- Being used or abused
- Drug use and drinking
- Teenage pregnancy

Just to think that as a kid, I thought being told no was the unkindest thing. What comes because of *no*?

- Hugs
- Appreciation
- Understanding, life lessons, and reasoning
- Bonds with family
- Game nights

- Dinner eaten together with prayer and hand holding
- Unconditional love
- Being a kid for as long as possible
- Sharing
- Consideration of others and their feelings

Finally, I got a *yes*—maybe that yes should have been a no.

My first time being able to ride my bike off the block with my brother, I turned a corner, trying to catch up with him, and rode into a moving police car. I was OK, but I wished at that moment I had stayed on the block.

Finally, I was old enough to get dropped off. Going to visit family had been fun when I was only there for a short visit. I soon realized that it was not what it appeared to be, and I was ready to go home. I had to wait to get picked up. That solo visit was the longest visit of my life.

Have you ever asked to stay the night over at a family member's house but then, when it happened, you realized the house had no rules, no set mealtimes, no bath time, no locks on the doors, and you couldn't sleep because there was no order? "Yes, I am ready to come home." That was the last time for that.

We all have family who live in the hood. I couldn't wait to get there and feel like I was part of something dangerous. When I finally got there, I had to step over people and walk the stairs because the elevators were broken. Nobody else noticed the posed junkies or the drunks staggering. The sound of police sirens blared all through the night.

This is all exciting until you understand that life doesn't have to be this way and that it shouldn't be this way; their parents should have told them no at some point.

Why do I now think this way? Because of no. I was protected from those negative things in life. My parents did a fantastic job of protecting me and preparing me for the real world at the same time.

Sorry, Not Sorry

It was once said to me, "You are the man your father raised you to be." My response was, "You mad because he raised me to know what a man should do and is supposed to do, and if you can't do it, keep it moving." I was also raised to know what a woman should expect from a man and how she should always be treated, not just when something is wanted from her. I have the best of both worlds.

I've come to realize people are full of negative energy. They'll realize you don't need them and you still have the ability and drive to get things done. Do it. Be your own cheerleader!

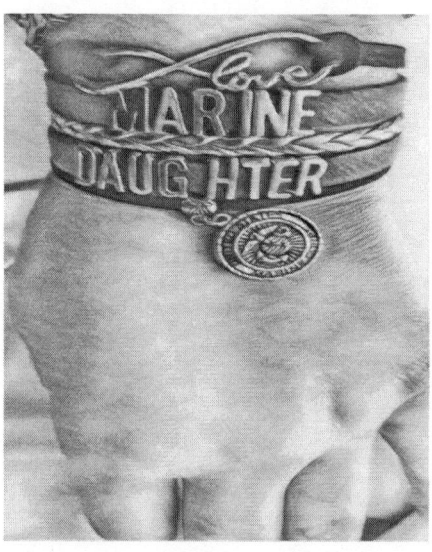

Wedding, Not Marriage

I don't know how I knew or why I felt like I never wanted to marry. I shared a vision with my parents. In my vision, I was walking around the deck of the pool in the backyard and marrying myself. It was the whole to-do—wedding gown, family, friends, food, a live DJ, everything that getting to the altar consists of. I married myself, just to say I did it.

As a child, I wanted a man to treat me the way Daddy treated Mommy and vice versa. I realized as a child that it takes special people to merge two different lives together. When two adults discuss their kids, what to purchase, or when to make a purchase instead of just doing whatever it is one wants to do, it says a whole lot to me. I thought the purpose of becoming an adult was to make your own decisions.

As an adult, I have never lost sight of that, and I continue to search for it. I've got to tell you: I have not seen too many relationships that have come close to my parents' relationship in my eyes. If there comes a day when I choose to take this marriage path, trust me: that guy is going to be something special to have a special woman such as myself. Until then, decisions are mine and mine alone, and I'm OK with that.

I Was Quite the Younger Sister

Pick and point. "I'm not touching you."

We all have played this game with family or friends. My version of "I'm not touching you" was sitting as close to my brother as I possibly could. I would hold my finger close to the center of his nose to make his eyes cross. This would be the highlight of some of my days. I just could not understand why it bothered him so much. After all, I wasn't touching him. If I hit him and ran, he was mad, and when I sat next to him and reached out to touch him, not actually touching him, he was mad.

He just sat there. Someone please explain to me why he sat there. I would laugh to myself, knowing he was getting more irritated by the second. Happy times before all the growing pains.

Bright Days—Sunny and Hot

As a child, I never wanted the sun in my face, but I loved the beauty of it. We had a vegetable garden growing up. I liked the thought of planting the veggies and watching them grow. Once they were in full bloom was when I had an issue. I can clearly remember Mommy calling home before she left work, saying, "Before I get home, you and your brother pick a bag of green beans and a bag of curly kale."

"Yes, ma'am."

Well, after I picked the bag of kale (easy picking), I would tell my brother, "Mommy said pick a bag of beans before she gets home." This was showtime for me. "I'm hot, I'm so hot, I'm sweating."

I couldn't wait to hear him say, "Go in the house, Dee. I'll get it."

Yes, finally I was relieved, so in the house I would go, still managing the process from inside and giving him a countdown so we would be done before Mommy or Daddy came home from work.

Now that I think about it, maybe I'm only here because he was such a good baby and toddler. The parents thought they would have another him—not so fast. I arrived, the "woke" child, never wanting to go to sleep. Mommy and Daddy said I would fall asleep and then, when I realized I was asleep, I would sit straight up in the bed and cry. The proof is in the pics—they have pictures of me in bed, sitting up, with tears running down my face and my eyes shut. Maybe I was just nosy.

Let me Go

I don't know who came up with holding someone's head and watching that person try to hit you, knowing damn well their arms aren't long enough. I call it the "arm to head" hold. I shed many tears in this position. This here, my friend, is complete torture to any kid. If this has never happened to you, ask around. You'll see the frustration of others without having it done to you. It's like being held hostage, waiting to be freed.

Nasty but True

So, a friend of my brother's tried the "arm to head" hold. I can remember being so mad, and my only option to be freed was to spit on him. I thought this was the funniest thing ever but unknown to me, Daddy was in the kitchen window watching.

"Come here" is what I heard. I got popped in the mouth. That laughter of mine was short lived, but I tell you what: I never had my head held like that again. A simple "Don't do that again" would have been enough, I think.

No Touching

I would play football with my brother and his friends all day. As I got older and more developed, he made it clear there were limits. I went from full contact to two-hand touch, and next was flag football. After that, I could no longer play, and I became a cheerleader. Thanks, Brother. No free feels for anyone.

Should Yes Have Been No?

A nice sunny afternoon, Mommy and I decided to go to the market. I just wanted to ride there and had no interest in going inside. I remember asking, "Can I sit in the car and wait?"

Mommy said, "Yes, and do not get out of this car."

I said, "Yes, ma'am," in my cheerful voice. Well, I thought if I didn't get out of the car, I was doing what I was told to do. I played with the door open, door shut, window up, window down. Mommy came out of the store, put the bags in the car, and off we went, no seat belt included.

Mommy turned out of that parking lot onto Reisterstown Road. Lo and behold, I found myself hanging on to the window by my fingertips, digging into the crease where the window comes from. It was as if I had just jumped into an amusement park ride and Mommy was the conductor. She slowed the car down and reached for me all at the same time. Mommy pulled me into the car safely. Finally, the ride was over. You would have thought I was trying to enter the birth canal I was so close to her for the remainder of the car ride home.

I must say for the balance of that day, I felt so loved and important. Thinking back to that day, I wonder if *no* was the best answer or if *yes* was a lesson to learn.

Choices ~ 9

Fun or Silent Pain

As kids, we all know there is no jumping on the bed. I had just got a new bedroom set with a brass headboard and egg-shaped caps on the ends. I had watched my parents put this together, assuming it was safe and secure. Not long after having it, I decided to put it to the test.

The first couple of jumps on the bed, all was well, and I didn't get caught. There came a day when I went a little too far. I jumped, fell forward and, reaching for one of the caps, that cap came off, and I hit my chin where the cap had been. I paused for a minute to see if anyone had heard it. I cried silently, trying to stop the bleeding.

Next, I had to tell Mommy I was hurt. Mommy calmly said, "I told you not to jump in that bed," as she was taking care of my cut. Lesson: Even though she didn't see it happen, she still found out I was being hardheaded. I still have that mark on my chin.

Expect the Unexpected at Grandma's

It was always so much fun to see Grandma. I never knew what to expect, but I knew laughing would be involved.

On this occasion, Grandma cursed out her neighbor who lived across the hall, and about five minutes later, she told me, "Go knock on his door and tell him I need a cup of sugar." He answered the door, and I repeated what Grandma had said. Without hesitation, he got the sugar and gave it to me. Grandma opened her door as I was approaching, and she said to him, "Thank you, you fat punk." He laughed, and so did I.

Ten-Minute Meals

It was nothing to watch Grandma make a cake or lemon meringue pie in the blink of an eye. To sit and watch her beat egg whites until they turned white and foamy was amazing to me.

On this day, Grandma said she was going to make an apple pie and told me to peel the apples. I tried to peel them the way she wanted, but I was cutting way too much apple. She looked at me and said, "Get away from my table." Thinking to myself, *Now I know how to get out of this task in the future*, I replied, "Yes, ma'am."

This was short lived. She called me back into the kitchen, then asked me to peel potatoes. Giving me a potato peeler and all, Grandma was ready for my nonsense this day. She had forgotten she had the peeler, but it didn't take her long to remember.

A few weeks later at Grandma's, while we were just hanging out, she told me to get a bag of apples. I was excited at first because I knew she was about to throw down in the kitchen. Then she gave me that damn potato peeler. I was trying to figure out a way to get out of this. I took the tip of the potato peeler and started digging into the apple. When Grandma realized what I was doing, she told me to get away from her table *again*. "Yes, ma'am." Mission accomplished. Needless to say, Grandma never told me to peel anything again—back to just watching and enjoying the fruits of her labor.

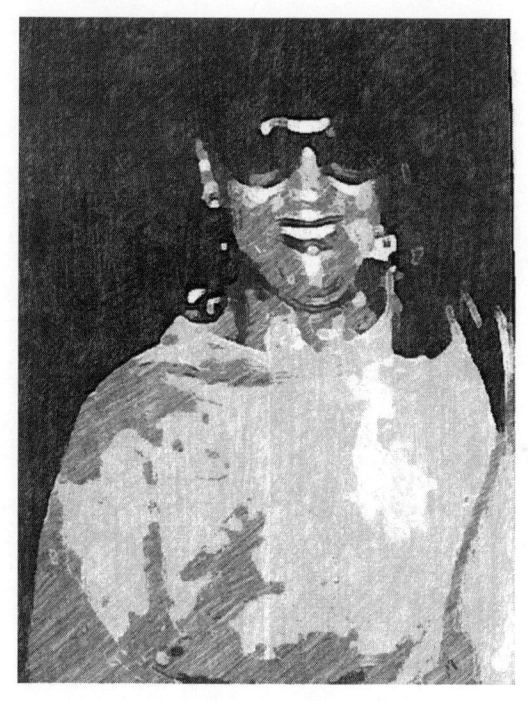

Choices ~ 13

Take and Give

Grandma was so sweet and comical, even a robber loved her. My first time taking a friend to meet her, I told him, "You are in for a treat." Guess what? Grandma never let me down.

After the initial greeting, Grandma looked at me and said, "Do you notice anything?" "No, ma'am," I replied.

Here is where it gets good. I looked over at my friend and said, "Don't say a word." Grandma said, "Don't look at him. You know this furniture is smaller than what was in here." I said, "Huh, what do you mean, Grandma?" She looked me in the face and said, "They came in here and took my furniture and brought this little-ass furniture in here." I said, "Well, at least they gave you something." Then I looked at him and said, "Don't say a word."

Bonding Time

Have you ever felt like you just wanted to hear your mom sing you a song—didn't matter what, just sing? Well, I have and still do.

Mommy and I were sitting at the dining room table. I said, "Hey, Ma, can you sing me a song?" She shyly responded, "What do you want me to sing?" I said, "Anything." Lo and behold, Mommy belted out, "Boom, boom, ain't it great to be crazy", nodding her head and swaying. I joined her in swaying; I wanted to hear more.

We both were laughing. I was laughing because I had asked for this, but who knew it would be a boom-boom song. Mommy was laughing harder and continued this song. "Boom, boom, ain't it great to be crazy, a horse and a flea and three blind mice were sitting on a curbstone shooting dice, the horse slipped and fell on the flea, the flea said, 'Oops there's a horse on me.' Boom, boom, ain't it great to be crazy?

I didn't know what I had just heard and why I hadn't heard it before, but we laughed so hard. I never found out the rest of the song, but I could tell Mommy couldn't wait to share it. As you can see, I was listening carefully and recording. I wish you could hear this song the way I did.

Daddy, Tell Me Something

I wanted to know why Daddy gave Mommy his money every time he got paid. I asked him how he worked all week and then put his money on the table. If looks could kill, Mommy would have buried me alive.

Daddy started to answer. Mommy said, "That's bill money. Don't you have what you need?" She went on a rant. "I pay bills with that money, girl." Her face read, *Mind your business, little girl.* Daddy's face lit up as if to say, *I was wondering the same thing,* but without hesitation, he said, "Mommy pay the bills and I just keep enough for gas and lunch."

In my eyes, it wasn't fair—you earn it, you keep it. Mommy chimed in again, making sure I knew she paid the bills, and even said, "Don't I take you shopping?" "Yes, ma'am." I still hadn't caught on enough to know to stop talking. I said, "Can't you just write a check?" I thought a check was money. Write it out, and done deal. I was so used to seeing Mommy with a pen and these blue checks when we went shopping, I thought that was the payment.

I never discussed their money again, at least not anytime soon.

Let's Go Check on Grandma

My parents had recently purchased a television for Grandma. I went to see her a few days later. I had a friend with me.

After we got to the house and relaxed for a few, Grandma said she needed an antenna. I asked, "What kind of antenna?" She said, "Rabbit ears." "Rabbit ears, what is that?" I had no idea what that was, but she made it clear. "Exactly what I said—a rabbit-ear antenna."

So now I was investigating what was going on behind the TV with all these cords. I saw the cord coming through the wall. I said, "Grandma, this is your antenna right here. I'll just hook this up to the TV; you don't need a separate antenna."

Grandma said, "Don't tell me what I need; do what I said."

"Yes, ma'am."

As I grabbed my purse to go to the store, I asked one more time, "You said *rabbit ear?*" My friend jumped in and said, "I know what it is."

Two stores later, we found this antenna. When we got to the house, ready to connect it, Grandma said, "They are watching me through the TV."

I said, "Who, Grandma?"

She said, "Your father and the government."

I looked over at my friend, shaking my head. I said, "Daddy."

She said, "Yeah, they all are spying on me. That's why black folks don't have any business; what all we don't tell, they see it through the TV and watch us anyway."

I didn't know what I had missed or what had happened while I was gone. I continued to hook up the antenna and then said, "All right, Grandma. I'm about to leave. I'll see you later." I am sure my friend had plenty of questions to ask, but he knew to just keep quiet and enjoy the ride.

Let's Get Cooking

Daddy had taken out a whole chicken from the freezer for dinner. We were preparing to cook for Mommy to give her a break. After all, Mommy worked and deserved to have a home-cooked meal prepared for her too.

Finally, the chicken was thawed and ready to be cut. I was standing to the side, watching Daddy dismantle this bird with a knife and man hands. He handed me the leg quarter and told me to cut the drumstick off. Picture this: I was standing there, turned sideways, with a knife in my hand. I must have sniffed loud enough for Daddy to hear me because he hadn't noticed the tears. He said, "What's wrong with you?" I responded, "It's still bleeding, and this doesn't feel right." All I could hear him saying was "Bless your heart, put the knife down." I couldn't get out of that kitchen fast enough.

A few minutes later, Mommy walked in the kitchen, and I could hear him telling her what happened, adding, "I didn't know she would cry." I wasn't in there, but in my mind, Mommy gave him the "you should have known better" look. I never had chicken duty again.

Gimme the Money

Another Friday. We know what that is—payday. Money is on the table again.

This Friday, Daddy called me to the table. "Count this," he said. First thing I did was separate the money according to the numbers on the bills. Next, counting the money, I stacked it in stacks of $100 and turned the bills in different directions. As I was counting, he was watching me, and Mommy was watching TV. I was nervous.

Now they were having a full discussion—about what, I didn't know, but they were trying to see if I could count correctly and listen. This was getting harder by the second. This lesson was "pay attention to what you're doing." I messed up my count. Daddy laughed because he knew I was nervous. The wad of money was larger than my little hands could hold. I was trying to count, stack, listen, hold it all at the same damn time.

After about seven or eight times, I finally counted it correctly. Then Daddy took the money out of my hand and mixed all those bills together and said, "Count it again." This time, he added an additional fifty-dollar bill. Let me tell you something, a fifty-dollar bill is the devil. I counted this money wrong again. I had to count it until I got it right.

Choices ~ 21

After I had been counting for what seemed like a lifetime, Daddy said, "Now take that money with you to bed, and give it to me in the morning." You can only imagine the pressure I felt holding on to this money knowing it was for bills and shopping. I could not let Mommy down. I didn't sleep much that night. I was worried that if something happened, it would be all my fault. I was so happy to see daylight so I could give him that money. *Now I can get some rest.*

The lesson, of course, was learning to count, and also not getting overly excited about money. I received the lesson, and to this day, I refuse to allow money to control my emotions, life, and circumstances. I have an appreciation for it, but it does not run my life.

Trying to Be Grown, and Caught in the Act

Walking around the neighborhood with the older girls made me feel like I had finally made it! Crossing the intersection of Reisterstown Road and Northern Parkway (the same area where I dangled from the car), the girls and I decided we wanted to dance. Everyone got a turn to walk and dance to show what they could do.

When it was my turn, as I was dancing, I heard a familiar voice: "Now dance yourself home." I thought I was hearing things, until Daddy pulled up beside me and said, "Get your butt home now." "Yes, sir," I responded, scared to death.

That was the longest walk home of my life, not to mention I was so embarrassed. That walk was the walk of shame. Although I walked slow, I knew not to take too long and keep Daddy waiting.

That was only the second spanking I can remember getting. I can still hear the words, "Move your hands," and "This is for your own good." I should have kept my ass on the block and played hopscotch or something.

Choices ~ 23

Going for a Ride

"Hey, Ma, can we go for a ride?"

Mommy and I would take our rides to nowhere. We called this place "Gatlin." I can't tell you where this name came from. Mommy was a good pretender of names and fantasies. Neither of us knew where or in what direction we would go; all I knew was Mommy was driving, we had gas, and I was out of the house.

Once a month, we would take our rides, enjoying our time together, and act out commercials. As we pulled up next to a car, we would pretend to ask if the driver had any Grey Poupon. Maybe the next time we would role the window halfway down and say, "Could you please pass the jelly?" An all-time favorite was seeing a guy standing at a bus stop and asking him, "Are those Bugle Boy jeans you're wearing?" no harm intended, just having fun and laughing the whole time. One thing about Gatlin—it was never the same place.

Driving in the Snow

Boy, was this going to be an adventure. Picture this: it was about dusk, snow and ice were covering the main streets, and traffic was backed up. Mommy decided she was going to take a detour uphill. We'd never traveled this road, not even to Gatlin. Mommy thought she was going to beat the traffic somehow. The only thing beating traffic was my heartbeat. The car was sliding side to side and backward. We sat still for a while; I'm guessing Mommy had to gather her thoughts and take a mental break. Mommy placed her hand on mine and said, "We'll be home shortly."

We made it home. It didn't seem to take as long as I thought it would. Did I mention we were in a 1985 Chrysler LeBaron? Ole Betsy pulled us through!

Family Time/Circus Car

At one point, Mommy was the only one of her sisters who had a car. On game night, everyone would come over to the house with their kids, normally two or three aunts and four to six kids. Every now and then, an aunt would leave early, but that wasn't often. So as the night went on, the discussion would be "Who is sitting where in the car?" "Who's getting dropped off first?" "Who is sitting on whose lap?" "Who is too tall to sit in the back?" We had to plan how to pack the car. This was a serious moment. My brother and I would want to ride as well so Mommy didn't have to drive back alone. We had to take turns. We couldn't both go.

The whole ride, all you would hear was "Get off me," "Move over," "Your knee is in my butt." Whoever was outside when we pulled up to my aunt's house was in for a show. This was the circus car of all cars, because of not only the number of people unloading but the fact we were laughing and joking about it. We laughed at ourselves. Mommy and the aunts may have had a few sips while playing games, so that made it funnier. After the first stop, if we didn't get in the car in the right order, we had to redo the process. Trust me, each stop had its own scenario. Our family game nights were so much fun and memorable inside and outside the house.

Daddy's Turn to Drive

As a kid, I thought one of the best hangouts with Daddy was the intersection of Fulton and North Avenue. There was a fruit cart and the clam stand, both pulled by horses. I could watch the horses and eat at the same time. Daddy's favorites were the oysters and clams. I just sat there watching the man shuck and stack them on a plate, waiting to see Daddy put hot sauce on them and tilt his head back. I would watch the clam or oyster slide into his mouth, and wait one sec to see him spit out a tiny piece of shell. This was the routine.

Eventually, I got my chance to get a taste to see what it was all about. All of you clam eaters know how small the muscle is. Daddy would cut that off and let me have that. Finally, I was part of all the excitement, hanging out with Daddy and on the scene!

Some Things Just Stick (Random)

A comment or fragrance may mean nothing to some and may arouse a lasting memory for others.

I used to watch my grandmother crack eggs and pull the "white string" off. She never explained why she did that; neither did I ask. I just followed her lead.

As a young'un, I found going to my aunt's house refreshing. Her house always smelled like powder. After walking around her house to find the source of this scent, I discovered it was Coast soap. Yes, even today when I smell that scent, I think of her. May God rest her soul.

Driving with a Purpose

Unlike Mommy, Daddy had a goal, lesson, or story to go with the journey of driving. Once, we were out driving for a while and ended up in Cherry Hill. Daddy began to explain the paths to take once you enter this community. The wrong turn would lead you out.

As we were driving, we saw a blue bus parked in a wooded corner. Daddy explained that was the store. "Yes, baby, we would walk back here and get our food and snacks." This bus was hidden off the main street, but necessary for the locals. This was like something you would see on TV. Daddy went on to explain that times were different then and he wanted me to experience a little bit of his upbringing in person, not just through hearsay.

You had to know when to keep quiet and just listen to the point Daddy was making. My conclusion: That place meant something to Daddy, perhaps a feeling of accomplishment, meaning he and Mommy didn't have to raise their family there or go through the obstacles of his upbringing. The lesson was to appreciate what you have because you don't have to walk in someone else's shoes. When people speak, just listen, and don't judge.

Random

"Ma, why is Daddy and my brother dark? Does it come off?"

Mommy immediately shut that down and said, "Don't say it again. People are all shades."

Kids think it and ask it—I got my answer. The end!

Let the Church Say Amen

Not so fast.

One Sunday morning service, I heard the pastor say, "Bastard," and explain what a bastard is. Hearing the church pastor say a word made me think it was as good as gold. He had my full attention. I wanted to make sure I understood the word so I could use it correctly.

Later that day, I called my brother a bastard. Mommy said it wasn't a nice thing to say and wanted to know where I got it from. I told her I had heard the pastor say it in church. I figured if the pastor said it, it was all right for me to say too. I said it a few more times on different occasions. Mommy said, "Don't say it again." She didn't give a damn who I had heard say it. By the look on her face, I knew she meant it.

Before this topic was over, I took one last shot and said, "According to the Bible, I am the only one of my siblings that is not one of those."

Pictures Speak Volumes

Have you ever seen an old picture of yourself and it made you feel like you were back in that moment?

Well, let me tell you, there is a picture of me at about four or five years old. I am in a red snowsuit with white fur around the hood, lying on my back in the snow. There are no footprints around me. Perhaps I was thrown out the back door to measure how deep the snow was. I asked about this picture and how it happened; all I got was a lot of laughs.

There is another picture of me in a pink terry cloth romper at the Baltimore Zoo. The sun is bright. I'm smiling and frowning at the same time while sitting on a cast-iron lion. The longer I look at this picture, the more I can feel the heat of this metal. Who thought of this? I bet it was Daddy.

Daddy could set up a prop and tell you how to pose and want you to smile on demand. There is a picture of Mommy lying on the couch in a blue evening gown, magazine ready, only this couch is covered in clear plastic. I'm sure it was a sticky situation, depending on how many scenes were involved. Every time we come across this picture, we laugh, and Mommy is sure to say, "Your father told me to do that," blushing the whole time. All I can think to myself is *I love the love they share.*

Mommy Shy? No Way

Mommy was not shy about posing and pretending either. Mommy had a green vase with a long skinny neck and a wide round base. On any given day, while we were sitting around in the living room, she would appear in an *I Dream of Jeannie* costume while holding this vase. We had our own genie in a bottle. For the life of me, I don't know how this happened or where it came from, but you couldn't tell me my mother didn't come out of that bottle. From time to time, Mommy would randomly ask if we wanted to see Jeannie. Mommy just wanted to be in costume for the family.

Locked In

On a nice spring day, the parents and I were out doing yard work. Mommy made a trip inside the house, Daddy walked to the front of the house, and I was moving chairs from the gazebo, placing them in the grass area. Well, I walked into the gazebo, and this time, it locked. I was there yelling, "Ma!" "Daddy!" "Mommy!" "Daddy!"

Just then, Daddy walked toward the end of the yard near the gazebo. I said, "Daddy, I'm locked in." He responded, "You what?" I repeated, "I'm locked in. I can't get out." Daddy said, "How did you lock yourself inside and the lock is on the outside?" "I don't know, but can you let me out?"

Now, I was thinking to myself, *Why are we talking about this through the screen instead of him letting me out?* I could feel myself about to have a full-on anxiety attack, which was crazy because technically, I was still outside. As Daddy unlocked the door, he said, "Only my baby could do something like that. I just want to know how you did it." He acted like I had performed magic. It was funny, but at the same time, I was anxious to get out of there.

How Strong Am I?

I had a nice workout at the boxing gym. Heavy bag, speed bag, jump rope, a little bit of weights, just an all-around good workout. I packed my bags afterward, went to the car, and put the bags in the trunk. And then I unlocked my door and pulled the handle off. I was proud of myself. I felt so strong. I called Mommy and Daddy to tell them. I called them for everything, strong and weak moments. I had to let them know the business.

I eventually crawled in the passenger side. At that moment, it didn't dawn on me that I would have to spend money to get this fixed. At the time, all I knew was I had bragging rights for something I'd never heard anyone else speak of.

Bigger than Life Itself

To every little girl, her father is bigger than anyone else. "Come on, Shorty," I heard Daddy say. "Yes, sir." He didn't have to call me twice.

As I told you, Daddy drives had a purpose. I didn't know where we were going and didn't care, but I felt like we were going on a secret mission. We jumped in the car and pulled up in front of this house that wasn't too far from our home. We walked on the porch, and the door opened; Daddy hadn't even knocked. We walked in, Daddy holding my hand. This house was dimly lit.

Once I looked up, I saw the biggest people I had ever seen in my life. Taller than Daddy, bigger than Daddy. I looked at these people from head to toe; even their feet were thick. As Daddy began to introduce these people to me, they reached out to shake my hand. Some gave hugs. I wanted to leave. They were all laughing with Daddy. He was enjoying himself. It was nice to see Daddy around new people and still being his bubbly self, but who were they?

Daddy finally said, "Dee, these are your cousins." "My what?" I was confused. Laughter filled the room, and Daddy, enjoying himself, made me comfortable. As time went on, I was looking at them and thinking they looked like my "real cousins" (the ones I already knew, I should say). The longer we were there, the more comfortable they were getting calling Daddy "Uncle James." I was thinking to myself, *This is for real*. I had to get used to hearing them call him that. I was only used to the "other ones" calling him Uncle. Now, I was about ten years old, so I had to get used to this, and of course, I asked a lot of questions. I was so confused at this point. "Are you …?"

You will meet them again. Trust me!

Turner Station

One way in and one way out.

On this ride, I learned a little more about Daddy's growing up and not having much. One of the stories that stuck the most was hearing Daddy talk about his mother's "boyfriend" who had to jump the rooftops when the Department of Social Services came knocking. The DSS would do home checks back in the day. A man was not supposed to be in the house with a food stamp recipient. I was a bit confused. Daddy explained a low-income family was given food stamps if a man was not in the home. In other words, if a man was in the home, he was supposed to provide for and take care of his family, not live there and live off the state.

Although we had more discussions that day, my mind stayed wrapped around the state's being involved with who was in your home. After a few more stories, we eventually made our way out of this circle and back home.

My lesson from this: Daddy did his best to provide, make sure our family stayed together, and not have the state get involved. Mom and Dad did an excellent job.

When You Think It's Over

It was a warm summer night. I was coming out 7-Eleven, Slurpee in hand. My friend was about to open the car door for me as I saw this black car that looked familiar. Not paying it too much attention, I glanced over again and heard my name: "Dee." I looked up. It was my uncle. "What are you doing out here this late?" "Getting a Slurpee," I said in my innocent voice.

My uncle ignored what I said and walked over to my friend and asked, "Are you the one who dented my niece's car?" Dude didn't know what to say. He'd never met my uncle, so he was caught off guard as well. I knew what each of them was capable of, so I was a little nervous. Dude slowly answered, "Yeah, but let me explain." Just as he said that, something inside of me said, *You are going to let my uncle punk you right in front of me?* My uncle cut him short and said, "Let me tell you something. No matter what she says, she's right, and no matter what she did or does, she's right."

At that moment, I was sitting on top of the world. Hell, he had kicked my brand-new car and left a dent in the front-right-quarter panel. Finally, it was addressed with fear, and I had the last laugh. Uncle came through and shut it down.

Choices ~ 39

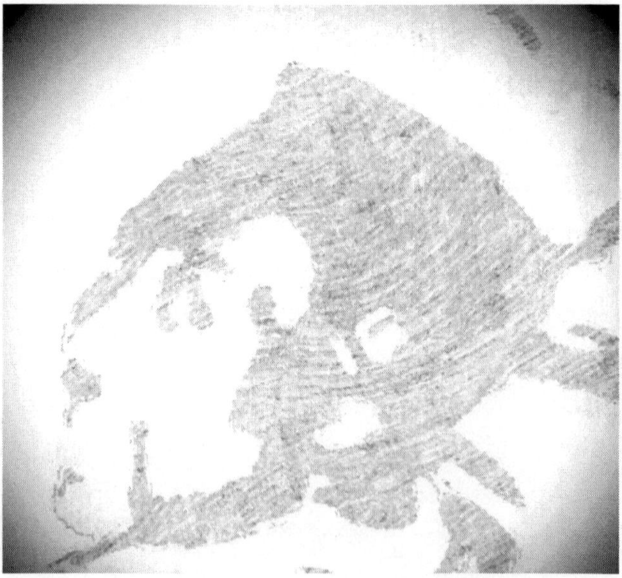

Repair or Stay Damaged

Speaking of this car, I had a cousin who was in the car business. Yes, y'all, I'm all about my family. I told my cousin that my fender was damaged. He said, "Don't worry about it. I got you." Now, I knew my cousin; this could go right or wrong.

About a week later, my cousin came to me and told me, "I have a fender for you." With it in hand, without a receipt, I looked at it, then him, and said, "No, you don't"—straight faced. I worked at an impound lot and knew car parts have serial numbers. I told him, "I don't want it." He asked me, "What am I supposed to do with it?" I said, "Get your money back."

He was so mad at me, but he understood it was not going on my car. We laughed afterward, but I know he was still upset with me.

And You Are?

Every year, there is an annual cookout at my parents' house. All are welcomed, family, friends, church members, anyone but kids—not at this one.

There was a new group I'd never seen before, and they were sitting in the center of the yard at the first picnic table near the grill. I was watching hard because newbies typically sit off to the side. But this crew was front and center and so close to the food. Greedy maybe?

Well, as time went on, more people were filling the yard, with music playing and just a great vibe. I kept hearing the newbies yelling, "Brother White!" *Brother White this, Brother White that.* When you call him, you are basically calling me too. So, Brother White, aka Daddy, sat down to talk to the newbies. By this time, I'd had enough of them. I said to my sister, "Those people at that table keep calling Daddy, and I don't know them." Again, *Brother White, Brother White.*

Well now, my sister was on point, and this yelling was bothering her because it was bothering me. She bossed all the way up, walking over to the newbies with her chair in one hand and cigarette in the other. While introducing herself, she asked them to do the same. Once she was satisfied, she told me they were new to the church and Daddy was the only one they knew other than each other. He had told them coming to the cookout would be a good way for them to get to know other church members outside of church.

Watching her get this information and politely excuse herself let me know she had my back and if something bothered me, it bothered her. Now let me explain. It's not that I was scared; my approach to people about my parents is a lot different from most. I have zero tolerance and I am not so low key—a little hood if you will. Sure, my parents know I'm no angel, but I never let them see me out of character; after all, I am baby girl.

New Car on the Move

Friends I'd met while working at the impound lot—two tow truck drivers—were in my neighborhood. I got a phone call. "Dee, what are you doing?" "Nothing much," I responded. "Are you home?" "Yeah, wassup?" He said, "Look outside." They were physically moving my car from one side of the street to the other.

By the time I put my sneakers on to run downstairs, they had already jumped into their individual tow trucks and pulled off. It was so funny. I was more impressed that they could do it than I was mad. I didn't have time to be mad about the move. These were the types of friends I had. Jokesters!

What Are You Wearing?

Well, what I can tell you is obviously Mommy thought it was OK for my brother to wear a belly shirt. There is a picture of my brother and me standing outside of a tent. I was clearly telling my brother something important, finger pointed at him as if to say, "Quiet." He was looking down at me as if I was crazy. As I look at this picture, I envision myself asking him, "Why can I see your belly button?"

There is a picture of my two cousins and me looking like triplets. As if we weren't bright enough, the flash from the camera put us center stage. The outfits we have on all are matching. We are either standing curtains, walking throw pillows, or flower beds. Picture this: denim jeans, but they look soft, with printed vests and floral sleeves and a floral print on the knees with our dirt-colored, reddish-brown hair in puff balls looking like pom-poms on the back of footies. It was a mess, but we were cute and still are.

The funny thing was when we got older, we all colored our hair black to get away from that dusty, dry-looking hair. Ladies, you know exactly what I'm talking about.

Close Quarters

Family came to stay with me for a few—nothing permanent, and shorter than expected. So, I had my cousin, "the fender getter," staying with me, and now my brother. We were all living in a furnished one-bedroom apartment. I didn't care about looking for furniture. Hell, if I could just move in, why not? It was small, but we were hardly there at the same times, anyway. Basically, we slept and bathed there.

My brother and I had our first real argument as adults. I felt like he was trying to run my house because he didn't care for my boyfriend. I made it clear, "Not here you won't." I called Mommy and Daddy and told them, "Y'all better come get him before I kill him." I don't know where this rage came from, but my parents came from West Baltimore to East in about fifteen minutes. Back to the White house, buddy.

Whatever the issue, it was resolved, and life went on. I'm sure you can think of a time in your life when something similar may have happened. I can't be the only one.

Choices ~ 47

Cousin Needed for Real

I had a burgundy 1985 Dodge Aries, my first car given to me by my parents. It was old, but I knew I was all that in my automobile.

One snowy morning, I made my way to the car. I got in and it didn't start. I called upstairs to my cousin, "Come help me!" Now as I told you before, my cousin was in the car business, so I knew he was gonna get me through this. I had to get to work. I was a waitress and had to open the store this particular morning. I called a cab, left my cousin the key, and let him deal with the car, in hopes he would get it fixed.

Well, that evening, he came to pick me up driving the car. As I approached him, I asked, "Did you find out what was wrong with it?" He said, "Yes," so I assumed he had got it fixed.

While I was putting my apron and bag in the car, he said, "Wait a minute, I gotta get under the car and I'll tell you when to turn the ignition." "What?" I responded. He said, "I know what's wrong, but I didn't get it fixed. It's easy: your starter went up, so you just need to hook part of a metal hanger to turn it." I said, "And just who the hell is gonna do this when I'm by myself?" He responded, "You can't, so you'll need me, and I'll know where you are."

We did this process for three or four days. He got up in the morning with me and came to my work every night until my day off, when I would get the starter replaced.

Random

What was Daddy really thinking? I was sitting at the dining room table with Mommy, felt like I was getting a sore throat. I'd just come from the barbershop and wanted my parents to see my haircut. I had a mask on to be sure not to make them sick if I was coming down with strep.

Daddy was on the telephone in the living room talking with my sister. Mind you, this was an open-area dining room and living room. I guess Daddy had forgotten I was sitting so close. I heard him say, "Dee just walked in here with her boy haircut." I thought he might have said, "She stopped over but isn't feeling well." Obviously, that was the last thing on his mind. This was my first mohawk; it was so cute, curly, and neat. He said what he said, and he meant it.

I looked at Mommy to see if she had heard what I heard. All we could do was look at each other and laugh.

Application Accepted

I had just received my work permit. In between basketball and volleyball practices, I found time to look for a job. I got a job on my first outing. I was happy it was not at a fast-food restaurant like most students'. Boy, was I excited; I couldn't wait to share my good news.

This day, Daddy made it home before Mommy. I could not hold the news long enough to wait for her to get home, so I told Daddy. "I got a job." He said, "You did what? Well, show me where it is." He was just as happy as I was, I thought.

So off we went. We jumped in his car, and he followed my directions. I wanted it to be a surprise, so I did not tell him the name. We pulled up to the gas station. I said, "This is it." Daddy looked at me in disgust and said, "Go tell those people you will not be working here."

I must admit I was so hurt. The whole ride home, he wanted to know why I wanted a job. I really had no answer. There was nothing I asked for and didn't get from my parents or my brother. I just wanted to have some say-so in my own life. Daddy made this discussion so short and unimportant it just faded away. His last words in relation to this were "Once you start working and making bills, it won't stop." I did not appreciate this at the time, but now I know it to be fact!

Fair or Not?

I always wanted to hang with my brother and neighborhood friends. There is a 4.5-year age gap between the two of us. So, when he was able to venture out, I wanted to go with him. I would ask, "Why can't I go?" The famous words of all parents, "Because I said so" or "You're not old enough," I heard repeatedly.

This day, I guess I'd had enough. I said, "It's not fair." Daddy responded, "Life isn't fair. If you think this isn't, wait until you are grown and leave this house. People in the world don't care about you or what's fair. We love you and know what's best for you." In all fairness to my brother, he would have put me in his pocket and taken me with him—most of the time.

Those words have marinated in my soul. If you allow the wrong people in, you will have long days and nights ahead of you. Life truly is not fair. Make your own "fair."

My Friend was Murdered Today

One of my best friends from high school—I never thought this could happen to a guy like him. Mommy called me at work and said, "He was killed last night and his sister left her number for you to call." I was immediately weak and sick to my stomach.

After speaking with the family and hearing the whole story, I could only think back to my parents' saying life is not fair. I am not saying he was a perfect person, but the wrong he did was to take care of his family the best he knew how. My friend was murdered due to jealousy and abandoned like trash. This was one friend I could say always had my best interests in mind, always.

I can remember a time when we were hanging out; he knew something was not right this night. He was on edge and told me to leave the area. It was as if something had snapped inside of him. "Dee, go home. This is not going to be a chill night." I tried to get him to leave as well, but he had something to take care of that was beyond my vocals. I knew it had to be serious. I had never seen him so persistent. I went home and called him later, and he told me he left not long after I did.

The next night, we sat out. I was drinking and talking about high school and the trials we all were facing, some self-sabotaged. We sat out that night until we fell asleep on the porch. He was just that cool guy that only comes once in a lifetime. We had that type of friendship that anyone we dated had to accept it. To think our friendship never faded until he was taken away from here.

I can honestly say he was the one person who proved my parents' statement, "Nobody cares about you like we do," to be wrong. He might not have had that parental care, but his was damn close. When I lost him, I tried as hard as I could to keep to myself. I never wanted another friend in life if I had to feel this kind of hurt. Our friendship was so genuine.

Family Pain

There's nothing like receiving a call in the middle of the night and finding out a family member is hurt. This time, it was my cousin—you know, the car repairman. I got the phone call: "Your cousin was shot. You need to get to the hospital." I disconnected and made my way to the hospital. My cousin had been shot over five times. I knew for sure we were going to lose him that night.

God is so good. He made it, although paralyzed from the waist down. It was a long struggle, and we all had to have patience with his impatience. Hospital to hospital, rehab to rehab, we were there to support him. We were determined to see him live his new life as comfortably as possible. Shout-out to our aunt, she received the brunt of all his frustrations but never left him hanging.

My cousin lived for about fifteen years after being paralyzed. I'm sure the only regret he had in life was being at that location that night. He certainly lived a full life, although it was cut short at age forty-five. I have nothing but good memories when I think of him; all I can do is laugh and cry at the same time.

Choices ~ 55

Pain on a Getaway

Mommy and Daddy went on a weekend getaway to the Poconos for her birthday, November 1. I always wanted to be the first to say, "Happy birthday," as the clock struck twelve. This year, I wanted to be considerate, so I called a little before twelve. After all, they were at the Poconos; maybe they would be having sexy time. Well, after calling and giving *hello*s, *happy birthday*s, and *I love you*s to them both, I went to bed.

About three minutes after speaking with them, a friend called and said, "Dee, your uncle was killed." My thought: *This is a mistake.* My uncle was too slick to get caught up in some bullshit that would harm him or the family. Once I sat up and got myself together, I knew I had to call my parents and tell them Daddy had lost his brother, his only brother.

I called. Mommy answered the phone in her happy voice, singing my name, "Dee." I said, "Ma, I have bad news. Someone killed Unc." Mommy had the task of letting Daddy know his brother was gone. Mommy and Daddy stayed the remainder of the weekend. They attended a costume party. People thought Daddy was Jim Brown. While they thought it was a costume, it was not. You be the judge.

Choices ~ 57

Fear in the Worst Way

This morning, I woke up to use the bathroom at 4:30. As usual, I had fallen asleep watching MSNBC or HSN. I remember so vividly a tsunami in Hawaii was the main story. I heard it, but it did not register completely. As I was getting back into bed, my eyes focused. There was a flashing red emergency report. I was sitting up in the center of my bed watching the water rise and trying to call my parents. By this time, I was in full panic mode. You got it! Mommy and Daddy were in Hawaii.

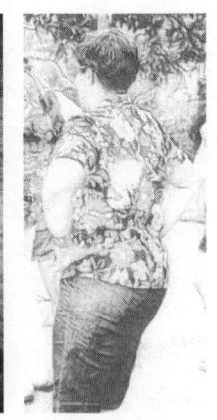

All I could think was *How do I live if both my parents die at the same time?* Mommy and Daddy had been there about two days at this point. I kept calling, getting their voicemails; the phones never rang. I was calling Mommy's phone, Daddy's phone, the hotel—nobody was answering. I was losing my mind. Now I was thinking it was my phone and all I could do was pray and ask God to keep my parents safe from harm and bring them back to me.

Again, after calling them for hours, finally the phone rang, but it was dead air. Now I was wondering if they were trying to call me and say their last goodbyes. The only updates I was getting were from the TV, stating people were moving from lower levels to higher floors, which did not mean a damn thing to me. I needed for the TV report to say, "Diana and James White are safe."

Steadily calling nonstop, I hit redial. Finally, Daddy answered and immediately said, "We are fine. I see you've been calling both of our phones." I said, "Daddy, can I speak to Mommy?" I just needed to hear her voice directly. Mommy said, "We were moved to another room, same hotel, and all is well. We lost our phone signal; that's why we couldn't answer you."

After speaking to them both, I felt a calmness come over me that was so relaxing. I thought, *What are the chances of me waking up to that and experiencing that kind of worry and relief in a matter of hours, one extreme to the other?* God is in control, and that was proven this morning for sure. I told Mommy and Daddy, "There is no escaping me. I will find you."

What I will tell you is love your parents together and as individuals.

To the Market We Go!

Saturday was supposed to be a day of chores and playtime—not anymore. Suddenly, I was part of a team (Mommy and me) to take Grandmother (my great-grandmother) to the market. Not just any market—one of the world's most famous markets. This was where you went to get all the fresh meat, fruit, and veggies.

I had never heard an order placed like Grandmother's "I want my ground beef lean" while picking out her own beef cubes to have them grounded. There had to be a certain amount of blood in the bag with the beef. At the next stall, she said, "I want my liver freshly sliced, not too thick and not too thin." I thought to myself, *What in the world?* and *How did I end up here?*

When Grandmother spoke, you just knew to listen, accept it, and keep it moving to the next stall because you best believe something else was coming and it wouldn't be long. Mommy and I were standing there like good soldiers. "Yes, ma'am" and "No, ma'am" were the responses of the vendors as Grandmother drilled them about the freshness of the food. After getting her meat, she was all smiles.

As we were dropping Grandmother off at home, Grandmother asked Mommy, "What are you cooking for dinner?" Mommy said, "Spaghetti and meatballs." Grandmother said, "Say it again." She was watching Mommy's mouth to say it correctly. As Grandmother tried to say, "Spaghetti," all she got out was "Spa." And the next thing I knew, her teeth flew out of her mouth, but she was fast and caught them midair and returned them to their proper place. Grandmother laughed and I was scared. I had never seen that before. We said our *see you later*s with hugs and kisses. I never heard her attempt to say *spaghetti* again.

Oldies Music

Walking into Grandmother's house on a Saturday night, you were guaranteed to hear some good old music. This day, I was not prepared for what was about to go down.

The first song: "Strokin', I be strokin'." I heard it, but I pretended I didn't. The next words were "Stroke it, Clarence Carter, but don't stroke so fast." I knew at that moment I was in the wrong room. Mommy said, "Grandmother, turn that off." Grandmother intentionally ignored her; I could still hear the music in the background: "If my stuff ain't tight enough, you can—."

That song came to an end. The next song was "Hello, Josephine, how do you do?" Grandmother shouted, "He's talking to me!" Josephine was Grandmother's name, so she had a real connection with this song. Grandmother was singing and swaying. She was feeling good. Now, I was about ten years old, give or take. I knew I shouldn't be hearing this. Here came another one: "Meet me with your black drawers on." I could not believe this was the same grandmother who sat in the living room praying with her rosaries in hand. I had a treat that night—"Hello, Josephine," "Strokin'," and "Meet Me with Your Black Drawers On"!

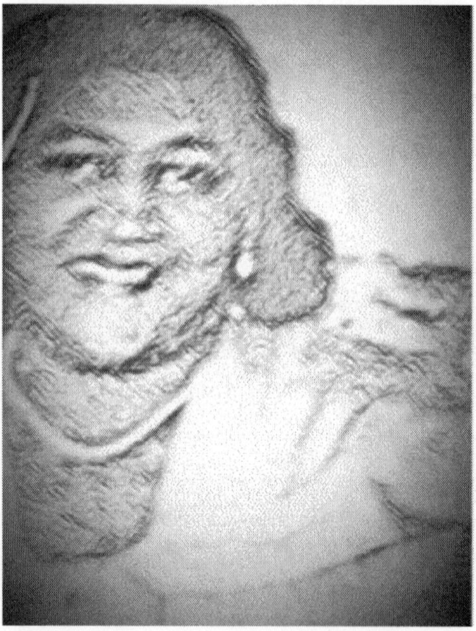

Missing Coins

From time to time, Daddy would say, "Someone is going in my car and taking my change; it's getting lower and lower." This went on for about a month. My initial thought was *If you know this, take the change out of the car.*

A few days went by, and Daddy called me and said, "Somebody has stolen my car." Daddy asked me about a few people and if I had seen them lately. I had not, but I will tell you he was dead-on with his assumptions. To this, I say when a person knows what they know, even trying to give people the benefit of the doubt or a pass, they still come back and try to steal your joy. All things done in the dark come to light, whether they're miles or states away. Daddy was proven to be right several times at predicting a person's capabilities and actions.

Family Affair, Known Meet the Unknown—Y'all Ready?

All the family I knew got together with the family they did not know. Yes, you guessed it: another cookout. This time, everyone was invited.

As the day went on, my "known" family asked me, "Who are *those* people?" I said, "They are our cousins," and kept it moving. The looks on their faces were priceless. It was funny to me. If they had taken the time to really look at them, they would have seen that we all favored one another, whether it was the same face, the same body shape, or the same laughter. We all had the same sense of humor. My "original" cousins wanted to know where these people came from. I could only answer with "They are Daddy's nieces and nephews." "What?" they responded. "Yup, meet your new cousins." Deep inside, I knew they would not ask Daddy; it was too complicated.

I knew a little bit but not enough to explain it clearly. I knew enough that something happened a few generations ago and our parents were left to piece it together and maybe even debate some facts. I kept my mouth shut.

We all got along and enjoyed each other's company. Some of the older cousins "new and old" knew one another from back in the day and were surprised to see each other. Daddy had not mentioned to either group that the others would be here—a surprise reunion within the cookout.

Find out who your family are and get to know them before it is too late.

How High?

My family didn't care for my friend, for good reason. Maybe they knew what was to come; I do not know, but I wish this were one of those times I said, "No, you cannot have my phone number." That's how deep the hurt would go. I wish I could go back to day one. I had no idea that drugs would be part of this relationship. I was hardly ready for that lifestyle and never imagined myself anywhere near it. There was something in me that I thought could save the world. You see, my parents raised me to help and be kind. When my boyfriend's friend told me he was getting high, I was shocked, but I thought I could help. *Wrong.*

I knew I had lost my mind and was in too deep. It was a Valentine's Day, and I was sitting in a detox facility. This jackass had called me and stated he needed help with addiction. I personally thought he was scared to come home because he had been on a binge, and this may have been the easy way out.

First off, when I got there, the people at the facility questioned me as if I were a damn junkie or a dealer. *Nope. Stop playing.* Once I finally passed the Q and A, they allowed me in the back. This was a pitiful sight to see, but I sat there and listened to the bullshit story.

As I was listening, the staff came around with hot cinnamon heart candy. *WTF!* I had tried to be the rock; however, my rock had been crushed so many times because he loved the rock.

To be continued …

Payback

Time passed. I found myself telling a friend from school what I'd been going through. I thought a good way to get my soon to be ex was to show him I had other interests. I let my friend drive my car around the neighborhood, where everybody knew us all. I got a kick out of that because I knew there wasn't anything he could do about it. He would not dare step to my friend. It was a respect thing. I wasn't worried about me. I could handle my own.

Once he heard about my friend driving my car, he knew our relationship was over. Of course, he asked me if it was true. I confirmed and let him know that my friend would always be my friend. I meant always. This dude would be part of me for a very long time, so much information shared and trusted as if we'd known each other from another life. We clicked like a seat belt! My ex had known about him and feared he was the one I would leave him for. He didn't like it, but he could see there was an unbreakable bond, all the while blaming others and not his addiction. I'm not saying what I did was right, but …

Insured and Spoiled

I parked my truck across the street from work. On my last break, I walked out to the lot to bring the truck into the garage. As I approached the vehicle, I could see broken glass; my truck had been broken into. Immediately, I called my brother because he was my go-to on most issues no matter what, only this time he didn't answer the phone. I panicked. The parents were in Jamaica, so I didn't want to bother them with my foolishness. I called my brother over and over—no response.

Finally, I decided to call Mom and Dad. They didn't answer right away, but Daddy called back in his cheerful voice. "Hey, baby, I see you called. Is everything OK on the home front?" At this very moment, I started to cry because I realized I needed my parents no matter how far away from me they were. I told him someone had broken into my truck, and I had called my brother and he didn't answer. Daddy said to me in a soft tone, "Did you call the insurance company?" "No," I responded. This next statement had me feeling so incompetent. "Baby, that's what you have insurance for." Daddy gave the phone to Mommy, and she told me what I needed to have available when I called.

Calling the insurance company had never crossed my mind. I had immediately gone into panic mode and called on who I knew to guide me and save me: family.

Not Enough Yet

Not long after the hospital drama and car ordeal, I found myself in another situation with this dude. I was relaxing at my parents' house. Mommy was in her room and Daddy was at choir rehearsal. Dude decided he was going to come disturb the peace. No sir, not at this house he would not.

I heard a light tap at the front door. My cell phone was ringing at the same time, but I ignored it. Something told me to go to the door. This bastard (a real bastard) was outside the house, picking up the stones on the walkway and throwing them at the door. He wanted my attention, and now he had it. I grabbed my coat and keys, never telling Mommy where I was going. I jumped in the car—you guessed it, the same little car with the fender bender!

I started my search. He'd already left. I had watched him ride off on a damn bicycle, so I figured he wasn't going too far, creature of habit. I pulled up on a side street near his family's house and waited to see if I would see him on that bike. It was dark, and I had on dark clothes, still in my security guard uniform. I got out of my car, got my baton out of the trunk, and put it in the sleeve of my parka.

I watched him ride his bike as if he had no care in the world. As he rode closer to me, I jumped from behind a tree. "Give me my damn phone," I requested. You see, the phones were in my name. Now I was in my feelings because he'd just come from my parents' house with the bull—! As he got closer to me, I let it be known, "Keep your distance."

Of course, a high person is not thinking rationally. Just as he reached for my arm, the baton slid down to my hand, and it was on. I smacked him upside his head, slicing his face. I took the cell phone and made my way back to my car. I had the nerve to talk shit and scared at the same time.

I got in my car and drove to my friend's house. I knew I wasn't going to my parents' because he would expect me to go there. Once at my friend's house, I explained to him what had just occurred. He cut me off and asked me if I was OK—he did not have time for the small talk. He had me go inside the house to get cleaned up. His concern was if I was hurt. I tell you I had the best friend in the world; he was already in the process of getting me a room ready to chill for the night.

While all of this was going on, Daddy called me and said, "Why did you do that to him? You cut his face." My first thought was *Why the f— did he go to my parents' house?* I said, "Daddy, why did he come to you?" Daddy said, "I don't know, but I told him he needs to go to the hospital." As I began to answer Daddy's question, I said, "Daddy, look at the walkway. He came to the house and was throwing the stones at the door."

I don't think Daddy agreed with my actions, but what was done was done. That was my last dealing with that bastard because I did all I could do for him and put myself in a bad situation, as well as others, especially that night.

Phone Call, and I'm Needed

"Hey, sis, where are you?" my brother asked me over the phone. "Up the street at the house. Wassup?" He responded with a question. "Have you been in the house?" At this time, I was living with my brother. I knew immediately it was time for me to roll. "Nah, but I'm on my way." My brother started to tell me something was missing from his house. I told Mommy, "I gotta go and see what is going on down the street."

So, I walked down the street. He met me outside with a look of anger on his face. I asked, "What is going on and what's the next step?" He said, "My shit is gone." Whatever *shit* meant to him; it meant something to me too. We were just that close—no stories needed. *"I need you to do ABC." "Consider it done."* So, I called my dude and said, "I'll be to pick you up in a few. I need you to ride with me." We had shit to take care of.

You guessed it again: I jumped in that same car, and we were on our way. I wonder why I was always the driver; it's not like they did not have cars. All I knew was someone had stolen from my brother and that was not cool with me. One thing about us, we were always there for each other. So we made our way to get the property, which I later found out was "my" property. I went along to get along.

After a little bit of confusion on how this property had ended up there, regardless of who it belonged to, we made our way back to the house.

For the Love of Crabs

Time passed after retrieving "our" property. I was on my way to get some crabs in the same area as the stolen property, but I was not thinking about that incident. I pulled up, went into the crab house. I was looking cute with my Janet Jackson braids, wearing a denim dress and my Converses, and made my way in and ordered my crabs.

After waiting a few minutes, I was walking back to my car with a bag of crabs in one hand and a root beer in the other. As I turned the corner, I saw people sitting on my car. I was thinking once they saw me walking, they'd move; they didn't. Next, I hit the alarm on my key chain. They still did not move. Now I was thinking, *This is about to get ugly.*

Suddenly, I heard a guy say, "Shorty, come get in the car." I thought, *They aren't talking to me; I don't know them.* I did look. Two guys were standing there just watching me. I continued to walk to my car. As I got closer, I could hear the confusion of "Is it her or not?"

At that point, I dropped my bag because this female was walking toward me and hit a bottle on the wall a few feet in front of me. The next thing I knew, she was swinging that jagged-edged bottle toward my face. I hit her elbow, causing the bottle to fly out of her hand. I could tell she was caught off guard.

I had to think fast, so I started walking backward. With my back against the wall, the two guys were still telling me to get in the car with them. I backed all the way into the crab house, and this group of girls was still moving toward me. One of the girls grabbed my braids as she pulled me toward her. My keys fell out of my pocket. Another girl stabbed me in my shoulder. I could hear the lady behind the counter screaming, and everything was happening so fast. I felt wet but nothing else. As I lifted my head, I grabbed the lid off a trash can in the corner of the store and started swinging it. The closest girl to me caught all the ridges of this top, and I watched her stomach split.

At this time, the lady was screaming, "You've been stabbed!" I honestly didn't think she was talking to me because I didn't feel anything. The lady opened the door, telling me to come behind the counter and that an ambulance was on its way. I wanted to know why she was telling me that. For the first time ever, I wanted the police.

Once she got me away from the commotion, one of the ladies brought me my phone and said a guy from outside had given it to her. As she was passing me the phone, it rang; it was my brother. I tried explaining to him what had happened. One of the ladies told him the location. He was not too far, getting there not long after the ambulance.

My brother called our parents. The three of them got to the hospital about the same time. My parents came into the room and asked what had happened and if I knew the people. I wasn't sure, so I chose to keep quiet; I had some investigating to do. I remember asking, "Who has my keys?" Nobody had them. My brother left to go check on my car. You know it, they had stolen my car.

As I lay in this hospital with a hole in my shoulder from a blunt object that had missed my lungs by less than an inch, I had all kinds of "get-back" thoughts. I had no feeling in my left side for hours. Once the doctors got me together there, and after dealing with the police, I was on my way. It was just a few hours later my car was found undamaged.

I don't know what happened between this day and the court appearance, but I wasn't ready to see *HIM* walk in with the other party. Could this have been one of those times I should have said no and minded my own business?

Another Midnight Call

Time had passed since the baton incident. I got a phone call at 3:00 a.m.

"Hello?" I heard nothing. I was about to hang up, but I heard this voice. "Dee, I'm not getting high anymore." I responded, "You must be high right now. Why are you calling me period, let alone this time of morning?" He repeated, "Just want you to know I am not getting high." I responded, "Good for you and good night," hanging up the phone.

Later that day, I got a telephone call at work saying he was dead. "Somebody killed him at about six this morning." That last conversation was replaying in my head, and I wondered if he had known or felt something was about to happen to him. Perhaps he wanted my last thought of him to be positive. I will never know.

Grilled Cheese, Anyone?

When I knew I was going to my aunt's house, I was excited—not just to see her and play in her shoes, but to have the best grilled cheese in the world, that good cheese you had to slice with the "good knife"! Don't act like you don't know what I'm talking about. I couldn't wait to see her cut that fresh cheese, melt that butter in the skillet, place the bread next, and start layering that cheese. I bet you wish you had one right now.

Another Foodie

I wanted to spend time with cousins I didn't see often. I don't know if the reason I didn't see them often was the age difference or the distance between our homes. But finally, I got to spend time with them. While watching TV, they stated they would be back, coming back with a sugar sandwich and a syrup sandwich, and asked if I wanted some. Nope! I had never in my life heard of these let alone seen them, and I for sure wasn't going to eat them.

Doll Head

I was always a tomboy. Perhaps it had something to do with a childhood experience.

I was about six or seven years old when I had a Barbie doll head. Just the head and shoulders. I had to sit on her shoulders to keep her still while doing her hair. Well, one day, I made my brother mad *again*! I can't remember all the details, but what I do remember is him throwing the doll head against the wall. The head split to the foam, and I took off running. That scared me to tears. I never asked for another doll like that again, only stuffed animals for me.

Stuck in the Snow, Turned to Mud

It was a cold winter night. I was just trying to get home from work. There was a traffic jam on the side streets, cars sliding backward and sideways.

To avoid this, I decided to drive on the sidewalk going downhill. Everything was fine until I pulled in front of my door. I'd moved on to a truck by now. As I was backing into the parking space, I lost traction. My truck drifted into a muddy ditch. I did all that I could to get out of this ditch—low, four-wheel drive, forward, backward. Nothing worked. My rear wheels were going lower and lower in the muddy snow. Then my front wheels began sliding on ice.

My truck started to smoke. Now I was worried. I thought these trucks were made for this weather. I called my tow truck buddies—yes, the ones who moved the car. They were on call, so I had to wait for a few, which was fine since I was home. One called me back and asked for my location. I told him, "My house." He said, "You just had to put your little truck to the test."

He came and pulled the truck out of the ditch. It would have made sense to stay on the street and not make my own path. Sometimes we learn the hard way, but at least I didn't have to pay. May God rest his soul, another friend gone too soon.

Ford Aspire

This was my first new car. When I had spoken to my aunt about purchasing a car, she had told me about the Ford dealer and their deals. I had made my way there and got this car on my own. I thought I was the *SHIT* (sugar-honey iced tea). No cosigner needed. I had no idea about interest and percentages or the length of time it would take to pay this thing off, and at the time, I didn't care.

After so many bad memories with the car, I didn't want it anymore. I woke up one day and decided, *This is the day I return this car.* I drove the car to the dealer, took my tags off, and left it. The service department called and asked me, "What do you need done to the car, because there was no repair slip." The service department employee also asked if I knew my tags were gone. I told him, "No, I do not need anything done, and I don't want it anymore, so I was returning it."

The finance department called me later and explained what would happen if I didn't get it and make payments. After trying to decide what I was going to do, I told them to do what they wanted; I didn't want the car. Fast-forward about two years: I started working my good job, benefits, and all, waiting to see this first check and, don't you know, my first paycheck had a garnishment. I could not believe it; they caught up to me just like that. Now I wanted to talk to someone. Too late!

Moral of the story: listen and ask questions. You can't run forever. Bills will find you. Daddy said life isn't fair. But to me, if you don't want something anymore, you should be able to return it.

Homemade Pizza

It was late on a Saturday night. The four of us were watching television. My brother and I asked if we could order a pizza. Mommy and Daddy had a saying: "You buy, I fly." I thought it was so cute. It didn't matter to me who purchased; I just wanted to ride with the flyer.

We always ordered the Sicilian pizza from Mike's Pizzeria in Pikesville. Daddy called to order, and they were closed. We were so disappointed. Our mouths were watering after the discussion of what we wanted on it. Daddy said, "I can try to make a pizza. Let me see what ingredients we have." As excited as kids could be, my brother and I couldn't wait to see this, or at least I know I couldn't. I was more excited to watch than to eat it. Mommy didn't say much; I guess she knew this would be another one of Daddy's creations.

The first item was a loaf of bread. *Wait a minute, what part is this?* I thought. But I was still excited. Then I saw cans of tomato paste and tomato sauce. I didn't know where this was going, but it certainly didn't look like any pizza I'd ever eaten—pasta pizza? Daddy turned the oven on, and placed that bread on a cookie sheet (once that got hot, it smelled like chocolate chip cookies). After mixing the sauce and paste, he smeared it on the bread. Next was yellow American cheese.

I knew this wasn't right, but after the grilled cheese with red sauce was done, we ate it and continued to watch TV. I can only imagine what Mommy thought about the homemade pizza. It surely was a sight to see. Parents do their best to make things happen.

Manual Transmission

I purchased a car I did not know how to drive. While I was working at the impound lot where I met my truck driver friends, one of their buddies pulled onto the lot with a Nissan Pulsar T-top. As you know, I'd left my car at the dealer, so I was on the bus, getting hacks (way before rideshare) and cabs for about two weeks. I had had enough of waiting on people and public transportation. I asked about the Nissan, and the guy knew I couldn't drive a stick. I said, "You're right, but I can learn."

After we went back and forth about this car, finally I got him to sell it to me under one stipulation: I had to prove that I could drive it first. I gave him my address; he came late so I wouldn't be on the street with other drivers. He was driving the Nissan and had someone follow him in their car. We drove to a quiet street but at a hill. He showed me what to do. I got in the driver's seat, nervous as could be, but I was not going to let that stop me from buying this car. The next thing I knew, he said, "I'll see you back at your house," and the two of them pulled off.

I was sitting there for a while. I had to build the nerve to pull off. I jerked my way up the hill, and the car drifted backward for a good ten feet. As I tried to take off, the car cut off. I tried again, and this time, I put the car in first gear but never stepped on the clutch. This was a disaster. Finally, I got the car started and in gear. Now the

Choices ~ 87

emergency brake was on, and the car was dragging. I had to stop and start this process over again. "Deep breath, Dee, deep breath," I repeated to myself. "Take the emergency brake off, left foot on clutch, right foot on brake. Start the car, left foot easing off the clutch. Give it a little bit of gas." I could not seem to get it together; my timing was off. Finally, I got it, and I couldn't stop smiling. I was determined to drive this car.

It took me about thirty minutes to travel what should have been a ten-minute drive. I pulled up to the house, and there they were sitting. The guy's friend said, "He never doubted that you would make it back." That made me feel good. I wanted this car so bad not only because I needed one but because my friend at the time had a 300Z and refused to show it to me.

Tough times don't last always. The next day, that car was mine, paperwork complete. I must admit I was still scared. I let the car sit for a few days. I had to build my confidence. Ever since that T-top, I have owned a car with manual transmission. I wouldn't change it for anything in this world. I can and I will!

Whose Daddy is Best?

About ten years ago, a coworker and I were discussing things we had done with our dads and continued to do. We shared ages, dates, and good and bad times growing up with our dads being there to support us, allowing us to make life decisions. My next comment to her was "I go to the gym with my dad four or five days a week." She responded, "Oh no, we don't do that."

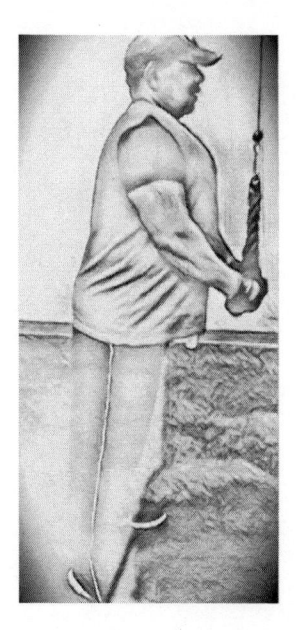

I went a step further and mentioned that he knew when my cycle was too because I got my 800 milligrams of ibuprofen from him. Her reply was "Oh hell nah, that's just going too far."

Just as we were talking, my dad called. I answered, "Hi, Daddy." She replied, "You win. My father doesn't call me." I thought that was perfect timing, so I was able to show her my dad really is the best!

My coworker and I became friends over this topic, silly but true. Not long after I proved my dad is the best, my parents had a cookout, and I invited her and her family. We immediately became family. You never know where a discussion may lead! This goes to show we can pick our family.

Repo

While I was working at the impound lot, there were coworkers, and then there were friends—great friends to me. One has passed on, God rest his soul.

The other tow truck driver called me one night. "Dee, what are you doing?" My response: "Nothing. Wassup?" He asked if I wanted to ride with him to repo cars. "Hell yeah!" I was always down for street fun with the fellas.

He came to pick me up at about midnight. I had my drink in hand, and we were off to the Palladium. While people were in there partying, we were outside looking for cars that would get him big money. I was trying to figure out how he was going to move those cars. The truck we were in tonight was different from the usual one. He didn't have to get out, just had to back up to the car, control the gears inside his tow truck, and pull the car from its spot. I was so excited because I knew this was dangerous, and I was ready for the excitement.

After circling the area two to three times, he spotted a car. Cars no longer had makes and models; he was calling them by tag number and the dollar amount he would get once he got it back to the repo lot. That didn't hold my interest. After all, that was his money; I was just company. I was more curious about how he was going to get to the center of these aisles. Cars were parked any way but the right way.

Before I knew it, the truck was in reverse, and we were shifting in an up-and-down motion. Now, I was scared. This shit wasn't funny anymore. It had just got real. What if someone came out and saw him snatching their car? The good thing was he never got out of the truck on the lot. Once he got the car locked in place, he would just say, "Got this money."

After securing the car and taking it to the holding lot, we went back. Even with all these cars on this lot, it was still like a ghost town, nobody outside. At this point, I was comfortable; my drink had done its job. I started asking him for tag numbers and searching for cars and counting his money. I was all in.

This next car was boxed in as if the owner knew something was going down tonight. Nothing stops a person on a mission, especially when money is involved. *Here we go again, tow truck in reverse.* I could see the car he wanted was in the center. I asked, "What are you doing?" He responded, "About to get this money." I said, "That is not the right tag." He responded, "I know, I gotta move these cars to get to my car." "Your car?" I asked. "Yes, the money car." All I could say was "Oh, OK." I sat there and thought to myself, *This isn't right. How could he move all these people's cars to get to the one needed?* I started thinking about the damage that could possibly be done to the other cars and the fact that the owners would never know how it had occurred.

Finally, he got the car and pulled it around the corner, only to go back. Now I was freaking out. "Why are we going back?" I asked. He said, "Dee, I gotta put those other cars back. You done got drunk and now you scared." I could not believe I was part of this.

We got the money car back to the lot, and he said, "That's it for tonight. I got my money." By now, it was about 1:30 a.m. The show was about to be over, but I was sure if he hadn't had to move so many cars to get to the ones he needed, he would have got more than two cars that night.

That night was pure adrenaline and alcohol for me. As he was taking me home, I told him, "Let me know the next time you go out." He said, "You got it," and dropped me off.

Family at Work

I once worked with my brother and our dad on the same base. We all had our own jobs, but Daddy, well, he had the good job—pipe fitter.

On my first day, I got to meet a few people my dad and brother were affiliated with. Boy, was this exciting, to see real men at work and in uniform, unlike what I'd been used to. After a while, I ventured on my own, looking for landmarks so I'd know how to get around.

On my first outing alone, I saw a man ride by. I had to do a double take, thinking to myself, *Man, he looks like my brother*. Still en route to try to find Daddy, my brother rode up to me and said, "I'll show you around," and I was thinking, *Thank God*, because every direction looked the same.

First stop, Daddy's shop. I was excited because now I got to see exactly what he did and where he took those great naps he spoke of. After spending time there, my brother and I jumped in his truck, and he showed me the main spots: bowling alley, gym, bar/lounge, cafeteria, and his office. Just as we were leaving his office, I saw that guy again. I said to my brother, "See that man right there? I thought he was you." My brother said, "I was looking for him earlier, don't you remember him from the cookout, that's our cousin." This was one of the new cousins I spoke of earlier. Small world.

Making a Person Question their Own Eyes

As I was getting to work one morning, the garage was still dim. I parked my truck so close to a column I could barely get out. The reason was parking was tight and the security cameras never seemed to work. I grabbed my bags and went on my way.

Later that morning, a coworker walked up to me and asked, "Why did you park so close to the column?" I asked, "What are you talking about?" She responded, "I saw your truck in the garage. How did you get out?" I said to her, "I have a red *car*," which I did, a red Toyota Paseo (five-speed). I went on, saying, "I don't know what you are talking about." She responded, "I just seen your red truck in the garage." Again, I said to her, "I have a red Paseo." She had a puzzled look on her face, and finally gave up and said, "I saw someone in a red truck before, and I thought it was you. Maybe it wasn't." I said, "Oh, OK."

Now, you may be wondering why I did this. People talk to you when they want to get in your business. Nosy and messy!

Choices

Vehicle or Work

At work, again. I asked someone a work-related question as we were leaving work, walking toward the garage. She told me that she would address my question the next day after she spoke with her peers. I knew this lady knew who I was by name because she worked with my mother, and in this place, nothing was private.

Moving on, the next day, another coworker asked me if I'd asked a different team the question I had. I responded yes. I was told their meeting opened with "A young lady getting in a big, pretty red truck asked me …" Because it was the same question, my coworker (friend) knew the person was talking about me, not to mention she knew what I drove.

My point here: people give unnecessary information instead of just moving along or asking what is needed.

What a Deal

I had been searching for a little car that I could drive every day—a gas saver. I found the perfect little car in a newspaper ad. I asked my girlfriend at work to ride with me to see this car. After we got off work, she followed me to the seller's house.

First, let me tell you this was the cutest little car, the red Toyota Paseo, five-speed, manual transmission. After the Nissan Pulsar, I was addicted to these manual transmissions. This dude wanted $1,500 for this car. It was worth it to me, thinking about gas and the car's low mileage. So, my friend and I got in and took it for a test drive.

After getting about a block away, I was thinking to myself, *Something is not right here.* All my friend wanted to know was why I had to do so much to make the car move. She was there for support and stranger danger, not as an interested party. I pulled up to the dude and told him the clutch was burning out. He immediately said, "I'll sell it to you for a thousand dollars. I need to get rid of it because I must leave the country." I probably could have talked him down a little bit, but hell, I was just as anxious to have the car as he was to leave. Deal.

I had that car for ten years. After I had the clutch replaced, it passed inspection. In ten years, I only had to get a new radiator and regular maintenance. Perfect timing!

Bright as Ever

This little car of mine, I wanted it to be different, but not sure how. While Daddy was in the process of getting his pickup truck painted, I wanted my car painted too. I chose the brightest yellow you could imagine. Daddy and I talked about it while at the shop with his truck.

A couple of weeks passed since we talked about it. I went to Jamaica for about five days and parked my car at my parents' house. Upon my return, not only was my car painted yellow, but Daddy had also added his own touch. He had the shop add glitter to the paint. This car was the brightest ball of sunshine you could imagine. In that car, if someone said they saw me somewhere, I had nerve to deny it. My windows were tinted so dark I could deny it because technically, they did not see me.

Make people think twice before approaching you. Stay ready!

The Youngest

I grew up the youngest, wanting to be the youngest yet wanting to be the big sister of somebody. I had a neighbor who grew up with me from about the age of five or six. We were always close, so close I referred to her as my little sister. The weird thing is people really believed it. We may have favored each other only because we were both light skinned with high cheekbones. So, throughout our school-age years, people fell for it.

One year for Christmas, we got leather puff jackets close in color, only mine was three-quarters length and hers was a hipster. This solidified to others that we were sisters. Looking back, I have assurances how shallow people really can be.

Fast-forward years—and I mean years, about twenty or so. My great-uncle passed away, and my "little sister's" father was at the funeral. Well, after speaking with Mommy, we found out we really are cousins through our great-grandparents. Regardless of how we are related, the bond we share is so real. Years have passed, and we pick up with discussions as if we spoke yesterday.

Remember, you can't choose blood relatives, but you can control your own circle of friends and make them family.

Kids and the Cops

I was about nine or ten years old when a bunch of us kids were outside on a summer day playing in the driveway and an officer was driving down the block, seemingly wondering, *Where did all these black kids come from in this Jewish neighborhood?* We were used to seeing the Northwest Citizens Patrol (NWCP) ride through but not the police.

The officer walked over to us just to talk. As he started talking to us, Mommy and our cousin Cookie could be heard singing through the window. The friendly officer asked, "Is everything OK in there?" Of course we were used to the noise, so we responded yes. He wanted to be sure all was OK before he left. We had to call for Mommy and Cookie to come outside before he would leave. They were so embarrassed all they could do was laugh and blame the terrible singing on each other.

The lasting impression from this encounter was police being nosy on the slide.

Mommy Retires—What an Event

Mommy and I worked together for eight years. Mommy was there way before I started. She had her own workmates, and I had mine. Nevertheless, I outranked everyone from the start; after all, I was the only one calling her Mommy. I started going to her desk every day for break, at lunch, and anytime in between if I could just to say, "Hey, Ma," and see her smiling face.

After eight years of us working together, Mommy had thirty-five-plus years, and she had had enough of that place. I didn't think she would retire. This quickly became one of the saddest days of my life. By my reaction, someone would have thought this was the only place I was able to see her. I was at my desk but could hear my coworkers around me saying, "Mrs. Diana is about to leave, and we're going to clap her out."

Well, I couldn't take it. I left the building and went to sit on the wall outside, where people normally went to smoke. I am not a smoker, but I could not handle the emotions I was feeling. One of my coworkers came outside to check on me, saying, "I knew your punk ass was out here crying."

After about thirty minutes or so, I knew Mommy had left; she isn't an attention seeker. I went back to my desk. I was sick to my stomach because I knew we would never have lunch together again at work. Only a few people knew just how close we were, but after this, it became obvious to everyone that Mommy is not just my mother but my friend. The minute I got off work, I went to the house, and we laughed about it, but I got what I went for—a hug, a hug from Mommy.

I gotta tell you no matter how much company I may enjoy on my lunch break, it has never been the same.

Grandfather?

I don't know much about my grandfather, but I do know he cared enough that he wanted to meet me. I met him at my high school graduation. After that day, I never saw him again. I guess he wanted me to know he existed. He died not long after.

However, I had a great-uncle on my mother's side who I often referred to as my grandfather, good ole Uncle Charles. Uncle was always at Grandmother's house when Mommy and I would visit. I knew he wasn't my grandfather, but I told Mommy I wanted to call him my grandfather. We laughed because I knew better, but he was

Choices ~ 103

the perfect picture of a grandfather. Although I always called him Uncle, behind his back I said Grandfather.

Fast-forward years later, Uncle passed away. My dad spoke at his funeral, and he said, "No matter what was going on when Uncle Charles spoke, what he said was the law." Hearing my dad say that was confirmation to me that I had chosen a great grandfather.

We *can* choose our family and the role they have in our lives.

Up All Night

Often Daddy couldn't sleep at night; as a result, he would order anything you could think of from the infomercials. You know how they say, "Order one and get another one free. Just pay separate shipping fees"? Well, at one point, this must have been OK with Daddy, or at least it worked out for me, because everything he got, I got it too. When I saw a commercial for night-vision glasses, I knew that Daddy would order these glasses; it was just a matter of time.

The very next day, I went to the house, and there they were on the table, my free glasses, in a plastic baggie. I said to Daddy, "I knew you were going to order them." He laughed and said. "They are yours." Daddy ordered cleaning supplies, cookware, gadgets, collapsible shoe racks, vacuum-sealed storage containers for clothes, car towels, Tommie Copper socks, and gloves and the list goes on.

One of my most memorable items was the rotisserie machine. Daddy gave me this, and I asked him, "What am I supposed to do with it since I don't eat meat?" His response: "Never look a gift horse in the mouth." My response: "Yes, sir." I took that Nuwave home, and to this day, I have never used it.

A few weeks passed. I was at the house, sitting there with Mom and Dad, and he had just got off the phone with the infomercial salesperson. The phone rang. Daddy answered the phone so aggressively. "Hello? Didn't I just tell you don't call me back unless you are going to ship it for free?" Now I was looking at Mommy like, *What the hell did I just walk into?* Mommy walked into the kitchen shaking her head and laughing. There was a moment of silence, and Daddy hung up the phone.

Not long after disconnecting the call, Daddy called them back, introduced himself, and said, "I placed an order earlier. If you all don't want to send me the free item without paying a shipping fee, then keep it." I looked at Mommy, and she motioned her lips: "Your father is something else."

There was a pause on Daddy's end. Then he said, "Stop trying to sell me more products and other offers. If you try to sell me one more thing, I'm going to hang up." Sure enough, that's what he did. Damn, if that phone didn't ring back. Daddy said, "Yes or no to my offer?" Daddy then gave his credit card number and said, "When we get off this phone, don't call my house anymore."

Daddy hung up the phone and started talking to Mommy and me as if nothing had happened. Finally, after a few minutes, he said, "I thought about all those $2.99 fees for shipping, and that was getting on my nerves." This was the funniest thing I'd seen or heard in a long time, but the lesson for me was to stand firm in what make sense (cents) to you.

Grown but Not Really

I'd graduated from high school and moved out of my parents' home and found myself pregnant not long afterward. Scared to tell Mommy for fear of disappointing my parents, but needing motherly advice, I finally built up the nerve to call her. I received all the love and guidance in the world, expecting good and bad, to be honest.

After our discussion, I asked, "Where is Daddy?" Mommy said, "At church, so you'll need to call back later." I responded, "Yes, ma'am." As I hung up the phone with tears rolling down my face, followed by snot, I was crying partially because I had to repeat these words, and also because I felt like I was letting my parents down. Luckily for me, Mommy softened the blow.

Daddy called me in a monotone voice. "Dee, how are you?" My heart was beating out of my chest. The moment I heard his voice, I began to cry. I did not have to repeat myself, thank God. Daddy said, "Your mother told me, and whatever you decide, I want you to know we are here for you." With my voice trembling, "Thank you, Daddy" was my only response. He quickly said, "Talk with you later."

At that moment, I was feeling sad because, I felt like I had let them down for the first time. God is always in control and knows best. Shortly after this, everything was normal.

Short and Disappointing

It was Daddy's birthday. Mommy and I decided to take Daddy to dinner, and I wanted my dad to meet my friend. Daddy knew him but had no idea I was seeing him—kind of a big deal and a surprise at the same time.

After we arrived to the restaurant and I greeted my parents with open arms in the parking lot, my friend took a few minutes to get out of the car. Finally, he caught up, hand extended to Daddy. "Hey, Mr. White." Daddy turned around, head high, and suddenly lowered his head to see who was greeting him. It was a funny moment, something from a comedy skit on TV. They shook hands, and we all had light discussions over dinner, nothing major.

After a few weeks, Daddy had had enough. "Dee, what are you doing with him? Y'all look funny together. I know the guys in the gym want to know what you're doing with him: 'How did he get her?' 'What does she see in him?'" Daddy ran all these things down, one after another. This was really bothering him.

I sat there in shock yet holding back laughter. I really thought it was a joke at first, but this speech went on for weeks on end. Daddy spoke on various topics about my friend—his wanting to appear larger than he really was and lifting weights and wearing tight shirts to make him feel taller, and also some spiritual differences.

After Daddy's constant reminders, I was finally seeing it for myself; he was right. The insecurities were starting to show even though I did not want to believe it. It was hard to believe this all started over Napoleon syndrome, and that was just the start. All the "shortcomings" were finally too much pressure. Nope, I was not having it.

I spoke to my cousin (China-Doll) about how I could not believe Daddy had serious issues with my friend over what I had thought were minor things but turned out to be deal breakers. When you think you like a person, you don't see what others see. In all actuality, there were major beliefs that neither of us could accept. My cousin and I laughed and said it seemed so wrong, but Daddy had said it from the start: "He is not for my baby."

When it comes to the way we view our own interactions with people, whether they be mates or casual friends, somehow our parents always seem to know best. Well, let me speak for myself—I wasted time, and time waits for no one. You're never too old to listen and be patient. That dinner surprise lasted far too long. "No more 'guess who's coming to dinner surprises."

The Famous Cookout Revisited

The drinks were flowing. Mommy's back was bothering her. I had Apple Pucker in my cup; someone else had Hpnotiq in theirs. Mommy decided she wanted to mix the two, she was walking around the yard saying she had Pucker-notiq. Mind you, she had taken 800 milligrams of ibuprofen.

My sister and I couldn't stop laughing while trying to keep her away from Daddy. He danced just about the whole night, while we played keep away. We knew he would want to know who had given her that drink. And in Daddy fashion, later that night, he said to me, "I know you and your sister gave Momma something in that cup she was walking around here with." I responded "Yup." Nothing got by Daddy; plus, Mommy exited the party, showered, and went to bed.

She's Known for That

Whether Mommy had her siblings at the house playing games or just the four of us at home, she would get up from the dining room table and say, "I'll be back." I was young but can remember this happening often.

As I got older, I came to the realization that her "I'll be back" was another way of saying, "See you all tomorrow." It mattered not who was there, how early or late; everyone was hip to her and would just say, "There she goes again." If the siblings were there, sometimes they would continue playing until they had enough and were tired themselves. I thought it was wrong to leave us, but when you're home and tired, why resist? Go to bed.

Daddy Did What?

As we all knew, Daddy had talent with his hands and could visualize a whole scene. We couldn't see the vision, but once he started, that was it.

For me, the ultimate was watching him go up and down this ladder building a gazebo with a broken ankle. Up and down the ladder he went, from patio to toolshed. And Mommy was his little soldier, walking boards back and forth for him, holding supplies, passing nails and screws, learning angles, and so on. Mommy may have been his assistant, but she was his wife first. "James, be careful." "Time to take a break." "Let's go eat." "It's getting hot out here." "We've been out here all day." Daddy would respond, "Honey, if you're tired, go ahead in the house." That was his nice way of saying, "I'm not ready to stop." When he would shut it down without a rebuttal, he was tired and knew he needed that break.

Of course, my brother was there to help also, normally on the days I was not there. You may be wondering why I wasn't helping. I was working two or three jobs at a time—yes, like a real Jamaican—and also trying to figure out this thing called *life as an adult*, always to return to open arms, knowing Mommy and Daddy would always be there.

What's Next?

The pool deck. After the aboveground pool was installed inground—yup, that's right, it's what Daddy wanted—he drew a blueprint for a deck. Once Daddy's mind was made up, there was nothing anyone could say or do to change it, total tunnel vision. There they were again, nails, screws, hammers, leveler, dirt, and more dirt.

Just so you know, dirt is not my thing. I will clean, build, measure, and swing a hammer, but digging in dirt is not for me. I helped with the deck but not enough that it mattered. My main reason for being out there was to be in my family's company and make sure they all had eight fingers and two thumbs each. I didn't really feel bad that I couldn't do much because I was working, taking care of myself and taking on too much and I was proud of my decisions. The running joke would be "What job did you come from, and what job are you going to?" I just wanted to prove to them that I was a diligent worker and was willing to put in the work and pay my bills—you know, just make them proud to know I was not lazy.

Life is rough once you leave home! This thing called *adulting* is serious business. I would comment on bills and work, and Daddy often reminded me of how I once couldn't wait to work, and for what? "I told you once you start working, you don't stop." The total truth. Mommy would be the voice saying, "Put something to the side," letting me know to save, even if it was just "a little something," and make sure I would not have to depend on anyone. Lesson taught and learned. I never asked her what "a little something" was to her—her little bit might have been a lot to me—but I got her point.

There are always small lessons that are taught throughout our daily discussions; we just need to listen more and talk less.

Mail

As a child, I wanted mail. I thought receiving mail was the coolest thing. But during mail call at the dining room table, only my name was never called.

One day, I heard my name. "Devona. Devona." "Yes?" I responded. "Something here for you." I was now legit. I was getting all the residential mail. Little did I know residential mail is junk mail; nevertheless, it was mine now. So now, I always had something to look forward to, but mostly on Tuesdays or Wednesdays.

Come to think of it, I don't know if my brother was receiving mail or not, but it seemed to me everyone who lived in the house should have been receiving mail, even if it came from school.

Time to Separate

It wasn't like you may think. There was a neighborly conflict that went too far, some may think. Daddy was hell-bent on "My yard is my yard, and your yard is our yard." He had suggestions for everyone, but if you wouldn't or couldn't accept his reasoning, he would say, "OK, OK. I tell you what, I'll just stay over here, and don't ask me anymore."

After days of blueprints and measurements, yet again, it was time to start digging and take several trips to Home Depot. Daddy could tell you where everything was there—what aisle to go to and which side to get something from. Off to the races, he went on his way to get boards, nails, screws, cement, and whatever else was needed to build this privacy fence. No more shared yard space, and for sure no more communication. One thing was for sure: once Daddy made up his mind, there was no stopping him or switching his beliefs.

Once the first slat was in place and secured, he never stopped until the project was complete, and he was totally satisfied. By *satisfied*, I mean the nuts and bolts were in and the fence would never come down unless someone used a boulder. Daddy said, "I hope I never have to take down anything I build because it's twice the work." He knew how much he had secured everything he built.

We knew at that point this would be the talk of the block, and there was no going back. Nobody outside of the "Whites' house" had thought the situation would come to this, but they clearly didn't know him.

My Turn at Home Depot

I received a call from home stating there was water all over my basement. I had to leave work and deal with this.

I got home and realized the water was still running. Lord have mercy, this dude couldn't even find the damn shut-off valve. After I shut off the valve sticking out of the wall at the bottom of the stairs, I started mopping up the water. At this point, I was disgusted and knew I was on my own as far as this cleanup and repair was concerned. Finally, the water was up, and I was off to the big store to find a replacement pipe for the one that had split.

Once I got to the store, I called Daddy. "Daddy, my pipe split in the basement. Can you please help me?" Well, this was the one time I knew Daddy was not feeling well; he had a head cold. He responded with "Send me a picture." I said, "I'm at the store." He said, "Nah, baby, you gotta go back home and take pictures so I can tell you what you need."

It was getting late, and I was under pressure. I went home and took what seemed like a hundred pictures from every angle, centimeter by centimeter, making sure not to miss a thing. I sent them to Daddy. Daddy said, "Write down what I tell you you need." Once I did that, I was off again to the big store. I got exactly what he said. He knew the aisle and shelf—he had this store down to a science. I was amazed by how he could picture this store and give such detailed directions. I made my purchase and was on my way.

After getting home, I felt complete disgust that I had to bother my dad while this man was just standing by—in the way, might I add—and watching. I called Daddy. "Daddy, I'm ready." As Daddy walked me through step by step, he asked, "Where is *he?*" and "What is he doing?" I said, "Right here," and "I don't even know. Why?" Daddy continued with walking me through this repair. As I followed directions, I was also taking pics to make sure I was on track. The final step was wrapping the pipe to make sure it was overlapping the other pipe and sealed properly.

"Turn the water on," he said. I was a nervous wreck. "Daddy, what if it isn't right?" He said, "Let it rip," and I did. Daddy believed in me, knowing it was done properly, more than I did. Like magic, I could hear water flowing, and not a drop leaked. I said, "Daddy, we did it, we did it." Another accomplishment under my belt. I may not be a pipe fitter, but for sure, I am the daughter of a pipe fitter.

Breaking Down them Walls

"Hey, Daddy, could you build me a breakfast bar in my kitchen?" "Build you a breakfast bar?" he responded. "Yes, sir. Just knock down the wall that divides the dining room and the kitchen. I want to be able to see the rest of the house from the kitchen."

A few days later, Daddy came over and took measurements. I knew at that moment a blueprint was about to appear. About two days after that, Daddy came over with tools, boards, and saws. He looked at me and said, "Are you sure?" I replied, "Yes, sir." Daddy said, "OK, let's get it."

Daddy took the hammer straight to that wall. I was so excited to see that first hole and the light shining through from the other room, reminding me of the movie *The Women of Brewster Place*. I was so happy. As the wall was going down, we discovered a hot pipe in the center of the wall. Daddy said, "What in the world?" I didn't think anything of it. I had all the confidence in the world that Daddy would figure it out. "Dee, I have to make a few adjustments." So that was it for the night. After Daddy left, I cleaned up a little, nothing much since I knew he would be returning.

Back the next day with a new blueprint, Daddy said, "Instead of the breakfast bar being one piece, I'm going to have to make it two pieces. One will have a curve in it to fit around that pipe." Daddy put those two boards together, a little wood glue underneath, and there it was—I had a breakfast bar with a heating pipe running down the middle. We shellacked the counter pieces. I painted the newly installed window frame / breakfast bar and even painted the pipe as if it were meant to be. Our job was a success!

After a few days of making slight adjustments and ensuring everything was secure, Daddy said, "I can't believe I didn't hit that pipe tearing down that wall. Dee, that's a heating pipe." Once he said that, I knew at some point during this project he must have been worried about what could have happened, but he never let it show. I have so much confidence in Daddy, I knew he would never start a project he knew he could not complete to his satisfaction. Another one under his belt!

Hungry at the Market

I can remember going to the market with my grandmother and a few of my younger cousins. We had to walk a few blocks to get there, and once we got there, we said, "Grandma, we are hungry." We wanted snacks. Little did we know Grandma would go all out. She said, "It doesn't make sense to be hungry in the market."

Grandma made her way to the deli counter and got some lunch meat and fresh rolls. Grandma made us sandwiches as she shopped. I didn't know if this had ever been done before, but I thought it was the right thing to do. One thing I always wondered about that day was this: Did Grandma pay for the meat and bread when she got to the register? Whether she did or not, no child should be hungry. Ever!

Shopping and Comedy

Mommy and I always had a close bond and our own means of communication. As I got older, when we would go shopping, people often thought we were sisters.

One day, this lady heard me say, "Ma." She said, "I thought you were sisters!" I responded, "Nope, that's my mom." Later that same day, we were in fitting rooms trying on clothes, laughing at the way the clothes fit the both of us. We were laughing so hard the other women in the fitting rooms were laughing. One lady waited for us to come out and said, "I had to see the two of you. You both had me laughing from hearing you laugh." Just as she said that, we looked at each other and laughed even harder and kept it moving. We were not there for personal entertainment.

This same situation has happened to us several times. I often wonder how many mothers and daughters or sisters who see us out together wish they had this bond that Mommy and I share.

Let's Talk about Parental Protection at Home

Have you ever tried someone's patience knowing you could get away with it?

I would hit my brother, knowing there was an endless hallway for me and an abrupt stop for him. *How?* you ask. I could run down the hall into my parents' room and dive onto the bed, but he could not. The minute he touched that carpet, he would know he had gone too far. You see, Mommy may not have been fully dressed, and Daddy was always dressed, so I knew that was my safety net if I had a running start. I could do this all day. The carpet was my security system.

Gangsta Mom

I'm thinking back to a time when Mommy shocked us all. My brother was in a bit of a situation and needed to get from down in the projects. My uncle was called, and Daddy was at choir rehearsal.

My uncle showed up, and while he was trying to figure out what was going on, Mommy popped up on the scene. There was confusion about what was happening, but what I do know is Mommy let it be known that she was ready to take care of business. We could not believe it. She said, "Yeah, I grabbed my piece and never gave it a second thought." She needed to get to her son, and nothing was going to stop her. I could not believe I had my very own Annie Oakley. I called her Mom.

Puppy Love

I found a puppy that I fell in love with. She was hardheaded and house-training her was hard. Mommy gave her a chance, but she didn't get any better. So, after a few weeks or so, Mommy let me know we were not going to keep her. We called the animal shelter several times for the exact location to drop her off; this was before GPS, Waze, and all these new navigation systems.

We went off to find this place. As we were riding, I was saying my last goodbyes to the puppy. We rode around for what seemed like forever trying to find this shelter. We ended up near Carroll Park. Mommy said, "Let her out. She should have to pee after all this time." I let the puppy out of the car and walked with her for a few minutes. Then I walked back to the car and sat down.

The minute I shut that door; Mommy pulled off. I immediately started to cry; I was so upset. Mommy looked at me and said, "Someone will find her and take her home. They'll be able to see she is well taken care of." As hurt as I was, hearing Mommy say someone would get the puppy made it easier to accept we had left her. It's amazing how your parent can hurt your feelings and comfort you at the same time.

When we got home, I told my brother. He could not have cared less; he had his own dog. So I told Daddy. Daddy had a story of his own to tell, about his dog Pete, who ran away. I was thinking to myself, *This is different from my dog getting dropped off at the park,* so that didn't help me. I wanted to be sad, but the family was not having it.

Fear of Fur

Christmas was in the air. Daddy couldn't wait to show me what he'd purchased for Mommy, even though this particular year we were not supposed to share what we'd got one another. We agreed we would all be surprised by what each other received. Daddy called me. "Hey, Dee, when you get off, come to the house. Everything is OK—just want to show you something." "Yes, sir," I replied.

When I got to the house, Daddy was so excited to show me this mink coat he had got for Mommy. "Try it on," he said. "I want to see how it fits you to get an idea of how it'll fit your mother." I said, "Daddy, I'm not putting that on." He couldn't believe it. He said, "What? What's wrong with you?" I said, "I can't." He couldn't believe I was not joking.

Daddy wanted to know what had happened to me that I wouldn't put it on. I said, "It just doesn't feel right." So, he tried another way. "Well, I got her a hat too. At least try that on." "No, sir," I said. I am sure he was sick of me and wished he'd never shown me. He might as well have waited until Christmas to show me as originally planned.

Fast-forward to Christmas day. After opening gifts, Daddy told Mommy about my not trying on the coat and hat. Mommy said, "James, I'm not surprised, and you should have known she wasn't going to put that on." He said, "Just to try, not wear, it." I made it clear to him I wanted no part of that fur on my skin.

Can you believe the very next year, he bought himself one and asked me to try it on to feel how warm it was? I thought to myself, *This has got to be a test. No, sir!*

Pool versus Beach

I watched my parents build around the house—swimming pool with the deck, add-on to the house, toolsheds, gazebos ... It was like a resort, a backyard getaway.

Mommy talked about going to Hawaii—again, along with other beach vacations. Daddy was not enthused about beaches any longer. I was thinking he was over traveling because he did so much in the Marine Corps. Nope, that wasn't it. I later found out it was a shark thing. Mommy said they were at Virginia Beach and he swore he had seen a shark and yelled for her and scared everyone on the beach.

Daddy later explained that was the reason he had put the pool in; he was trying to make the yard as comfortable as possible for Mommy, and she could have all the water she wanted. Mommy wasn't hearing that. She wanted beach sand and a real getaway from home. In case you're wondering, she got both!

Home Gym

Going to the gym was nothing for Daddy; however, Mommy would have no part in it. Daddy had two memberships and tried as hard as he could to get her to work out. Since Mommy wouldn't go, Daddy decided to bring the gym to her.

Buying exercise equipment was still a no-go. It started small—bands, light dumbbells (homemade ones that he made from steel), a stepper, and an under-the-desk cycle machine. Nothing was interesting to her. When I asked her to walk the track with me, she said, "I am not walking in circles to nowhere." Mommy knew that working out was not her thing. Daddy was determined to get her to move, and she was just as determined to keep still. He went as far as to purchase water weights to see if she would at least use those. Not a chance in hell.

Mommy is a reader and loves board games and cards—a little badminton or volleyball here and there, but that just wasn't enough for him. It's funny how a person can try as hard as they know how to get a person to find an interest in something. But if that doesn't work, hey, let it be. Finally, he did—for a while. Not long after, there was a treadmill, and another. He has never stopped trying.

Mommy Meant This

"Pay yourself first." "Always put something up for yourself in case something happens; I don't care if it's just five dollars a pay." "Have your own." I live by this. As long as I have enough room for me with a bathtub, I'm good,

Middle School—No Phone

I can recall one time, and I do mean one, a boy called the house and asked for me. Daddy answered the phone and asked him, "What do you want with her? Whatever you need to ask her can wait until you see her in school tomorrow." To make it worse, he said, "Do me a favor: don't call here anymore." I was so embarrassed. I did not understand the harm. Daddy had his reason, and I was not about to ask. That prepared me for high school. I knew what not to do.

In high school, it wasn't as bad as I thought. I played sports, so it was a given guys would be around me, and so was Daddy. He was as much a part of the team as we were ourselves. He got to know the girls and the guys. I didn't feel like I missed a beat as far as interacting with the guys. The fact that none of the guys had my contact info never came up because we spent so much time together during school hours, practices, and actual games. I never heard that speech again. Mommy never weighed in on this topic. I guess she felt the same as Daddy, and since I didn't question it, we didn't discuss it either.

Everybody Gets a Turn

When my brother and I were growing up, people were quick to judge and assume they knew things that were going on and how they would handle situations. They did not understand why my brother and I had so many restrictions on what we could and could not do, where we could and could not go. I often heard our parents were strict. I must admit I thought so too, compared to other households. The same people who said this to me now have children and understand parenting isn't easy and sometimes they all need a break.

Let's go a little further but on a light topic we all can relate to. There would be cookouts at the house, and no kids were allowed. Everybody who had kids thought this was so wrong. "How can we all come, and we all have children? What are we supposed to do with our kids?" Fast-forward a few years, not many. "I'm having a cookout, and no kids allowed. I need a break from my kids"—the people who complained are now doing the same things. These are the people who thought kids should not be corrected or punished. "They're being kids."

Kids my ass—correct them now and be friends once they are grown. People say I don't understand because I don't have any. You don't have to have a child of your own to know right from wrong and see that kids are on the wrong path, but hey, who am I?

Living the "Good Life"

Finally, I found a man who I thought was going to change my life. No more work for me—I thought I would sit at home, relax, and help raise his kids. Not married, I was ready for this life, or so I thought. You know how it is in the beginning: you think you love a person and are ready to help them no matter what.

After a few months, I found myself seeing my family less, and everything was all about my relationship. I was not realizing weeks would pass where I didn't see my family. Every time I got ready to leave, something would come up. The kids needed something, he had to go to work for OT, there was no babysitter—you name it, I heard it. Time was moving on; my family events were happening, and I was no longer part of anything. That was my own decision, but I was feeling like I was needed at home. What was I doing? Whenever something came up, I was taken shopping, collecting all this jewelry and clothes and going nowhere. Realizing what was going on, I had to get me back.

I started working again and making new friends. It took me several years to realize I basically had been kept for material possessions. Once I was able to get over that and party with family the way I was used to doing, he wasn't ready for this new "old" Dee. My first objective was to move and make my own home. I was no longer living in the shadows of the past. When I was ready to move, Daddy gave his input on doing it together or staying independent.

Growing pains sometimes hurt, but we gotta step outside of our comfort zone before someone gets hurt. That has always been my way of looking at things. We never want to do anything that could cause life-changing events in a negative way.

Love, Family, Birthday/5-0

Brother was in for a surprise this year. The family was giving him a birthday party / cookout all in one. I was in charge of getting his strawberry shortcake. Boy, was I in for a surprise of my own.

The night before the event, I had to get the cake. On my way to Little Momma's house to get this cake, I was pulled over by police in an unmarked truck. After my light turned green, I had to wait for oncoming traffic to stop before I could make the left turn. As I made the turn, they put their lights on, so I pulled over to let them go by. Well, don't you know they pulled up behind be. I didn't know what they'd seen, but I knew I'd done nothing wrong.

As I sat there with the flashing lights in my rearview mirror, the plainclothes officer was approaching my SUV with tinted windows, yelling at me to put my hands out the window. As I looked in the side mirror to see what was happening on the passenger side, I saw another officer was walking to the truck with his gun drawn, yelling for me to put all my windows down. I did as he requested. Again, the officer was telling me to keep my hands out the window. Now, I couldn't do both—but the officer closest to me on the driver's side was just close enough to notice my hands and fingernails. I believe my nails saved me from more drama.

The officer said to me, "Didn't you see my lights flashing?" I responded no. He went on to say, "Why didn't you go through the light to let me through?" I responded, "Because I didn't see any lights." This bastard looked at me and said, "Have a good night," and dismissed me. I was glad this ordeal was over, but at the same time, I was confused and upset. I know in my heart the only reason I was pulled over is because I was in that SUV with tinted windows and had on a baseball cap.

Once I got my nerves together, I continued to Little Momma's house. By the time I got to her house, I was a shaken mess. I explained to her what had happened and just sat there for a while. Never in a million years would I have expected anything like that to happen to me. I called my parents to let them know what had happened and that they should be expecting me back to the house in a few minutes.

After getting back to the house and telling them this story in detail, I was nervous all over again. I do remember thinking, *This is why these guys out here have no respect for the police*—NWA. Needless to say, the party was a blast. Food, drinks, family, friends, and that invaluable cake were all worth it. Brother was pleasantly surprised, and that's all that mattered, but trust me, I let him know that cake was something special with lasting memories.

Mommy's Turn

A party for Mommy on Halloween—what a treat. Mommy's birthday is November 1, so why not combine the two?

Both sides of the family attended, some in costume and others in regular attire. We had a few witches and skeletons there, highly creative. We had so much fun with all the *remember when*s. Mommy was a bundle of smiles and laughter. Each time the doorbell rang, her face lit up with a larger smile than the previous one. We had so much food it looked like a Thanksgiving feast. One thing about our family gatherings—we gonna eat!

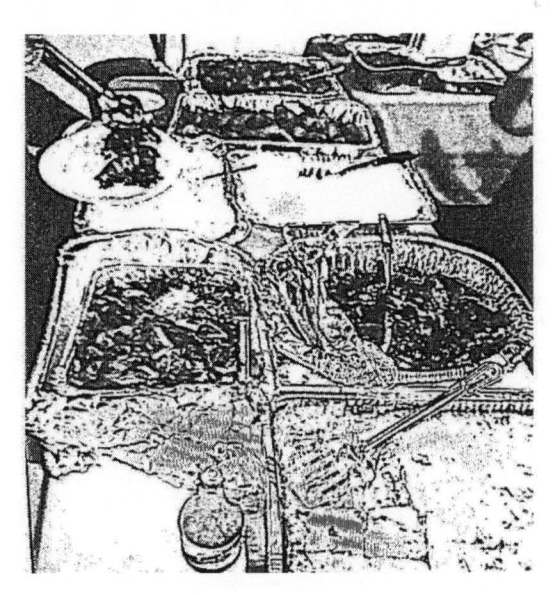

We had a toast to the birthday girl, and whoever had something to say, the floor was open for them. After Daddy shared his love and appreciation of Mommy, nobody initially wanted to follow him. Of course, I was in tears listening to the love coming from Daddy to Mommy, knowing I was a product of this love.

Those who did see me wiping my face had no idea part of the reason I was crying was I felt like my parents' love brought out the best in me and showed me what love is all about, come hell or high water. No matter what, they were united. I felt like every wife should have a husband who cares so deeply and will do what he can to make sure her needs and wants are met, and a wife should do the same, as well as support things that she may not agree with, but that's her man. I also felt like every child should have parents like mine, but not mine—sorry, mine are off the market. Call me selfish, but I love my best friends / parents, and everyone knows it.

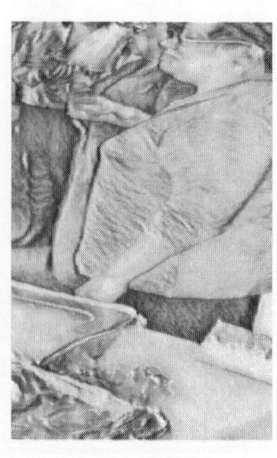

I See Your Hands

Periodically, Daddy would walk up behind Mommy in the kitchen and smack her butt. I could see when his hands were right about there, about to go in. *Daddy, I see you!*

This gesture disgusted me, and I mean to the bone. Sometimes it would be a long hold of cupping. That would drive me nuts. Although it was cute to see the affection was there, it grossed me out at the same time. Mommy would say, "James, you know Dee doesn't like when you do that." He didn't care. He would just turn and look at me and say, "What's wrong with it?" I really didn't have an answer other than "I'm going home." Sometimes he would say, "Oh boy, see you later," and then laugh. I knew they still had feelings and desires; I just hoped not when I was around, and not in the kitchen.

Daddy Gets a Surprise Too

We had planned a surprise birthday party, and we all were on snow watch. It snowed the night before and the morning of. We had a break in the snow, but there were about six to eight inches out there. We weren't sure the party would be possible, but everyone was still on board. We cooked and called one another to figure out a time to meet at the house. Here is the funny part: the party was at their house. Daddy wasn't going anywhere in the snow, so we had to be strategic with timing.

When we all got there, Mommy opened the door and said, "James is asleep." That was music to our ears. It gave us time to take the food into the house and get nice and warm. Daddy had no idea he was about to wake up to a house full of family and food. After about thirty to forty-five minutes of us being there, he called for Mommy. "Hey, honey, you call me?" he asked. She said, "No, but come here."

We were spread out in the living room and dining room. We could hear him walking down the hallway. "Surprise!" we yelled as he stepped beyond the hallway door frame. Daddy was so surprised he didn't know what to do with his hands—cover his face, wipe his face, or give hugs. His face was priceless. His first words were "How long y'all been here, and why didn't y'all wake me up?" It was so nice to see the look on his face as well as the family's faces. We politely told him we had wanted him to get his nap, but we had really needed that time to set up.

After the element of surprise wore off and he washed his face and all, he came back into the room with us. He said how thankful he was that we all had come out in the snowstorm to celebrate his day.

After we all shared our stories of how long it had taken us to get to the house and how we had almost had accidents, it was time to eat and celebrate. When it came time to sing "Happy Birthday," we realized in all the excitement we had forgotten the candles. Mommy found a 6 in the kitchen drawer, and Aunt B made a 4 out of a plastic straw. You can't get any more original than that.

We had so much fun. It was nice to see Daddy laugh so hard as well as look so surprised. It's hard to get something past him, but we managed.

Once the celebration was over, it got real. We were full of as much fear of driving home as excitement from sharing Daddy's birthday with him.

Choices ~ 145

Anxiety, Telephone Calls, and Money

I have anxiety and had it for several years not knowing it had a real name. At some point, I got used to it and just fell into a pattern. The minute my heart would start racing, I knew to put my pit bull named Reds in his cage and wait to see if it would pass. Once I realized it was not going away, I would call 911, and a few minutes later, I had company—the ambulance and the fire department. I didn't know what else to do. They would come faithfully, sometimes even knowing the door was already open, and there, I would be sitting on the couch, holding my chest.

After a few visits, one of the firefighters told me I could try to calm myself by grunting as if having a bowel movement, but not too hard, unless I was actually on the toilet; if not, I may need to change clothes. That was funny and helpful.

The EMTs would check my vital signs and then ask if I wanted to walk to the ambulance or needed the stretcher. By the time I walked to the stretcher, they would tell me my heart rate was back to normal and ask if I still wanted to be transported to the hospital. I did go a couple of times. This went on for several months until I started getting bills from Baltimore City. *I am getting billed for help?* I said to myself. *Unbelievable. Not anymore!*

I learned to grunt and pray at the same time. Sometimes, I couldn't do it alone. I would call Mommy and Daddy just to talk and allow their voices to calm my soul. I think deep inside, they knew I was upset or having some type of meltdown. It would be 1:00 or 2:00 a.m.; only sad or worrisome calls come that late.

This one night was a little different. I called; Daddy answered. We talked a little bit. Mommy was asleep. Daddy said, "I'll be over in a few minutes." I was so relieved the minute he said it.

I opened the door, awaiting his arrival. And in he came with a doctor's bag. That bag consisted of his blood pressure cuff, a diabetic monitor with strips, aspirin, and of course a singalong. He first checked my pressure, which was high sometimes, but that may have been the result of the panic attack. To assist with this, he asked, "Do you have vinegar?" Now I was rethinking what I'd got myself into. He said, "Pour a half cup of water and an equal amount of vinegar. Now drink it." I did.

While waiting for this magic in a cup to work, he checked my insulin level by pricking my finger and trying to get a drop of blood on this stick. Unbelievably, sometimes that was the hardest part. My hands would be sweating because of the attack. I was a mess. Once we got the blood, my reading would always be 104 and below. He said, "Your sugar level is good." I felt better, whether it was because of being in his presence or just hearing him say something was the correct number.

Now back to checking my pressure. While I was sitting there waiting for the vinegar to kick in, he sang gospel songs (his own) and walked around, admiring his work in the kitchen. After about a half hour or so, it would be time to check my pressure, and it would read normal.

Daddy said, "Dee, this is just a quick short-term remedy. Don't be in this house drinking vinegar and water like it's a regular drink." I responded, "Yes, sir." He knows me so well. We sat and talked for a few as he packed his doctor's bag. He said, "OK, baby. Daddy's going home, so we both can rest, and I'll call you to let you know I'm home."

When he got home, Mommy was awake and asked him, "Is everything OK with Dee?" He told her, "Yes, she's OK." Mommy knew exactly where he had been.

The next day at work, I told her the whole story from the first feeling of increased heart rate to the minute Daddy called and said he was back home. We laughed about the doctor's bag and how it had saved me from another bill, knowing just a few hours ago I thought I was going home to glory.

"Can You Come Over?"

I walked into my house and survived a nightmare. I just knew this was my last night alive. The one who I thought was my protecter flipped on me. This time it was alcohol and jealousy. I experienced about 30 minutes of rage. All I could do is my best to stay alive and protect my head. I finally made it to my keys. A bloody ass mess but I made it. After making a trip to the hospital bruises from head to toe, I got home and called on my friend. "Can you come over, please?" He knew I was in a relationship, and so was he. Never questioning me, he arrived and let me be. I wanted to be alone and wanted company at the same time.

One thing I can say is there was no pressure to talk. He just sat and waited as I tried to clean myself and the house. I showed him the bruises a little bit at a time. He never forced me to talk. Finally, I had a meltdown, and he was just there to comfort me.

When I think back to Mommy and Daddy saying, "The world doesn't care about you," I beg to differ. I have had some of the best friends a person could ever ask for. The one thing I didn't think about was putting my friend at risk. I don't think it crossed his mind either. The things we do for family and friends are lifesaving. I am forever grateful.

Game Night

Every so often, the cousins would have game night at one another's houses. This night, it was at my house. Dealer's choice, card or board games, we added shots—some kind of alcohol to make it even more exciting. Everybody came with a bottle. We know how we do. We could drink our own or somebody else's; it didn't matter as long as we drank something other than water or juice.

This night, I invited Mommy and Daddy over. It was their anniversary. I thought it would be something different for them to hang out with the younger crowd and see us in action. They never confirmed.

As the night went on and we were all getting wasted, there was a knock at the door—the good parents. Oh my goodness, we were all faded but somehow straightened up once they appeared. We played a few more games as Mommy and Daddy just watched and laughed at us.

The night was ending, and I decided, *One more round*. It was my turn. The game we were playing was like a tabletop pinball machine; you shifted the game to get the ball to fall into the pocket. I cheated. My beverage was telling me to use my hands, and I did. Now everybody watched me cheat, and I still took a shot. As my cousin would say, "One time for your mind."

The minute I swallowed that last shot, I ran to the front door (thank God we were on the first floor). I had just enough time to unlock the door, step out of it, and lean over the side railing. Everything I had that night and the night before appeared. I was so embarrassed. Not only had I never been drunk like that before, but my parents were there to witness it. All they said was "Mm-mm-mm. Good night, Dee, and talk to you later" (it was already the next day) as they walked out the door. My cousins and brother thought this was the funniest thing because I had cheated and caused myself to vomit, and my parents had got to see another side of me. I laughed later that day, but I never let them see me like that again.

Millionaires

I thought my parents were millionaires. Why? They had it all in my eyes. I never heard them say they wanted anything; I never heard them argue over money or discuss how a bill would be paid. On several occasions, I told them both, "I have learned the value of money. I feel like I am responsible enough and I am ready to stop working." That led to me asking them, "Can I have what y'all are going to give me now, because I'm tired of working."

Daddy said, "Bless your heart," and Mommy let out a laugh that was so contagious I laughed too, but I was so serious. I was tired of being around people, not being appreciated for my work. And hell, I just wanted to be left alone until I felt like being bothered by the outside world. They had enough for everything they wanted and knew how to save together. They watched me work two or three jobs at a time, so they knew I had hustle in me. They just didn't want to give it to me too young.

This went on from twenty to twenty-three years old. After a while, I had another conclusion: they wanted me to appreciate challenging work just a little longer so I wouldn't blow it the minute they passed it over. The lesson behind this: work hard, and common sense can lead to whatever you want.

Admiration/Confirmation

Not long after graduating, I moved with my cousin. We always had a bond, but I looked at her different. She was a single mother with a great job, her own everything. She dated occasionally, but let it be known, she could take care of herself. She did not take any shorts. I have never forgotten the talks we shared, and even to this very day, I live my life on a similar path minus the kids.

My confirmation came full circle. I was chatting with my uncle, and he said, "You remind me so much of your cousin," no name mentioned. But I knew exactly who he was talking about once he started stating general facts that could only be about her—not taking S.H.I.T. off these guys, speaking up for oneself, always being ready with an on-point response, taking care of business, and not being a pushover.

As Uncle was talking, my mind drifted. I was thinking, *Damn, that was over twenty-five years ago.* What a coincidence that he was speaking of her and me in the same breath. As far as I knew, he had no idea that I lived with her for a couple of months and that I really valued what she had instilled in me as a single woman dating: *Never be anyone's doormat. Nope! And remain self-sufficient or at least not dependent on a partner, and let him know it. Regardless of what he has, remember it's about you first.*

My cousin wrote me a letter telling me how proud she was of me and mentioning what small steps I was making at that time. I still have the letter—again, twenty-five years later. I needed to let her know I listened, I had heard her, and Uncle heard her in me as well.

Not More Than Me

I'd met a few friends over the years while working, never quite like this new one. I'd started a new job and had some coworkers tell me to watch her. Hell, I'd just started. I wanted to know why they were so comfortable telling me this. I treat people according to how they treat me. To me, she was genuine, but I did notice a little competitiveness.

As we became closer, I started to notice when I got something new, she would get something close to it, or even better. No big deal to me—I'm not that girl. I guess part of me only paid attention because the coworkers had already put something in my head.

I got a pair of diamond earrings from my parents for Christmas. After I wore them one time, she asked about them. I let it be known, "I did not purchase them. My parents gave them to me." Don't you know she went online at work and found them? She told me, "Your parents paid good money for them." My response: "OK." What do you say to that? About two or three days later, she told me she had opened an account to get the earrings, only hers were white gold; mine were yellow gold. I thought to myself she must really like them.

Time went on. And she did it again, but this time with something even more expensive, and higher risk. It made no sense to me, should I say. I was in an accident and totaled my Neon, so I got a Ford Explorer Sport. She traded her Volvo for something similar. Now my eyes were totally open. I could not believe what was going on. And for what, to say, "I have it too"? I told people, "Don't try to keep up with me; my parents are millionaires on the low. Half of what you see does not come from my account."

A few years later, after maturity finally set in, we became the best of friends. I think she was looking for acceptance, and once she realized I was not out for competition, she finally accepted herself for who she was and what she had or didn't have. May God rest her soul!

Weed, Work, and the ER

Now, I'm going to let you in on a secret. On my way to work one day, trying to be grown, I was smoking a joint. I don't know why, but I tried it. I was driving down Pennsylvania Ave, crossing North Ave and I started getting dizzy. It looked like the double yellow lines were shifting. I needed to keep driving until I could find a spot to just pull in.

I got down by the Billie Holiday statue and pulled over. I started shaking, and I was so thirsty my hands started to clench. I didn't know what was happening, but I knew not to call my parents—Mommy was already at work, and the truck smelled like weed.

I called my brother; he only lived a few blocks from where I was. I told him something was happening and to come to the statue and bring some water. While waiting for him, I made sure the weed would not be found. I was more worried about getting caught with weed than being saved.

My brother got to me with the water. But I couldn't grab the water. My hands were folded. I told him to pour it in his hand, and I drank it out of his hand like a dog—don't judge me! I believe he was as scared as I was; he called the ambulance.

Check this out: as I was getting into the ambulance, Daddy was riding down the Avenue. He got out of his car and asked what was going on. The paramedics said they were taking me to a nearby hospital. Now, I was in the ambulance thinking about how I was going to explain this. My brother and dad both were following the ambulance.

When I got to the hospital, the doctor asked if I was on drugs. I was too scared to lie. I said yes, I just smoked weed, but that was it. I was praying that they got all the questions out before Daddy arrived.

After talking to the doctor, I pulled out an energy pill from my pocket as Daddy was entering the room. Daddy said, "That's a yellow jacket. What are you doing with that?" I said, "It's a pill to help lose weight." Now I was looking at him like, *What in the world are you talking about?* A lot of communication was lost in that little bit of time.

The doctor then came back into the room and said I was severely dehydrated. They had me on fluids. My brother also came back to make sure I was OK. What a relief! I didn't have to explain the whole story.

I later asked Daddy where he had been going that early (he was retired). He said, "An appointment at the VA." That was my sign weed was not for me. Think about it; that was God's way of checking me using Daddy. Although the weight-loss doctor said to drink a lot of water with that pill, I wasn't drinking enough water, and the weed didn't help. So now y'all know why I don't smoke and haven't had a desire.

Even as an adult, I am still my parents' little girl.

People often ask me, "Why do you think everything is funny? Do you take anything serious? Do you care about anything?" Sharing my experiences, letting people know we all face obstacles of anxiety, depression, mental and emotional abuse, and fears, but that doesn't mean we have to get stuck there. We are given a new day to make another decision, hopefully better than the previous. When you have a great support system, family, and friends such as I had and have, you have all the reasons in the world to smile and really laugh out loud.

I really don't give a damn what people think about me. I am here!

Words I have lived by for years and try to pass along:

> "Don't let anyone steal your joy."
>
> —Daddy

> "You have to pray and have faith."
>
> —Mommy

> "Let that shit Go."
>
> — DeeVerné

As long as I have God and my parents by my side and in my corner, I can, and I will.

January 30, 1946–July 2, 2018

Daddy,

I wish I'd thought to put my thoughts and feelings on paper prior to your homegoing. The comfort is knowing I never missed a chance to say, "I love you," and talk with you literally every day. Thank you for all your music. I still get to hear you sing to me.

Missing you,
Dee

....So many sides of me, I'm not done yet....